HOW TO
MARKET & SELL
TO THE U.S.
GOVERNMENT

A VIEW
FROM THE
INSIDE

HOW TO MARKET & SELL TO THE U.S. GOVERNMENT

A VIEW FROM THE INSIDE

Brian Hebbel

ACKNOWLEDGEMENTS

I began this book in 2010 and it was almost ready for publication in 2012. However, due to numerous circumstances including my demanding career, growing family, and the declining health and subsequent death of my father, it has taken five years to publish this book. As a result, I want to thank my wife Janet for not losing faith in the completion of this book. Janet and my family have heard "the book" mentioned thousands of times over the past five years. In fact, I would not have completed it in 2015 without her and my family's love and support. I am a lucky man and have been blessed with a wonderful and supportive family. I truly appreciate the support and encouragement they have provided to help me complete "the Book."

CONTENTS

INTRODUCTION

This book is intended to help United States (U.S.) federal government contractors win contracts. Regardless if you are experienced or inexperienced in this field, there are certain tools and techniques that are required for marketing and selling to the federal government. In this book, I will describe the best practices you will need to gain knowledge, gather information, and develop relationships. These three areas are the keys to federal government contracting success. The first three chapters in this book outline basic information that a contractor needs to know to market and sell to the federal government. The subsequent chapters outline key marketing and sales techniques that will help your company win a federal government contract.

The information, tools, and techniques outlined in this book are often overlooked and some are never considered by experienced contractors. For the experienced contractor, this book will help "raise the bar" for your marketing and sales staff by providing what I consider key information necessary to effectively market and sell to the federal government. For the inexperienced government contractor, this book will help to level the playing field. Overall, this book will enable federal contractors to break down the barriers preventing them from entering the federal marketplace and winning contracts.

How do I know this? I have worked in federal government acquisition departments for over thirty-two years and I have institutional knowledge of the acquisition process from the inside. As a result of my long career, I have met hundreds of contractors. I have observed the difference between successful and unsuccessful contractors. As a result of these observations, I know the knowledge, tools, and techniques required by successful federal contractors. This book will get to the heart of the matter and present required information, marketing, and selling techniques to guide contractors on a successful journey in the federal government marketplace.

CHAPTER 1

GOVERNMENT CONTRACTING KEYS TO SUCCESS

The federal government has often been a powerful economic force that has significantly increased the Gross Domestic Product of the United States. The purchase of supplies and services for the federal government has often helped the economy in difficult times. This was true during the Civil War, the Depression, World War II, and more recently, the economic crisis in 2008.

The federal government became the 600-pound gorilla of the economy in late 2008 through 2011 as private sector sales dropped and small and large businesses began looking for the federal government to fill the void. Companies needed revenue generated from the federal government to increase their corporate sales; in some cases, they needed the federal government revenue just to stay profitable. As a result of this trend, a greater number of small and large businesses are looking to access the federal marketplace.

Even though private sector sales have been weak in the past decade, the federal contracting marketplace has remained strong. USAspending.gov provides a lot of information regarding government spending. In Fiscal Year 2003, USAspending.gov reported federal contract awards for all departments and agencies totaled 318 billion dollars. By Fiscal Year 2008, it reported an increase in federal contract awards to 542 billion dollars. In Fiscal Year 2014, it reported federal contract awards decreasing to 443 billion dollars. As a result of the significant and

1

continued federal contract spending, the federal government remains a lucrative marketplace.

The Department of Defense (DOD) significantly exceeded all other federal agencies in contract awards in Fiscal Year 2014. USASpending.gov reported that the DOD had 284.9 billion dollars in contract awards in Fiscal Year 2014. The next closet agency in Fiscal Year 2014 was the Department of Energy. It had 25.4 billion dollars in contract awards. The Department of Health and Human Services had 21.4 billion dollars in contract awards in Fiscal Year 2014. The DOD remains the goliath of federal agency spending.

Large commercial companies substantially benefitted from federal contract sales in Fiscal Year 2014. USASpending.gov reported that Lockheed Martin had $32 billion; Boeing had $19.4 billion; General Dynamics had $14.5 billion; and Raytheon had $12.4 billion.

Small businesses also substantially benefitted from increases in government contract awards. The SBA has reported that in Fiscal Year 2005, $75 billion were awarded to small businesses. In Fiscal Year 2011, $98 billion in contracts were awarded to small businesses and in Fiscal Year 2013, $83.1 billion were awarded to small businesses. The Small Business Administration (SBA) sets a goal of 23% of all federal contract awards dollars must go to small businesses. The SBA website reported that a 23.39% goal was achieved in 2013.

Various states also benefitted from the federal government contract sales in Fiscal Year 2014. USAspending.gov reported that Virginia had $52.1 billion; California had $45.9 billion; Texas had $29.2 billion; Maryland had $27.7 billion and the District of Columbia had $18.8 billion.

If you are looking to access the federal marketplace or increase your federal sales, this book will deliver proven techniques to help you achieve your goals. It will provide you the key information, tools, and techniques to help increase your corporate sales and/or access the federal marketplace. If you are an experienced contractor, I will guarantee that it will provide you with information, techniques, and best practices that you have never considered. It will help to break down the barriers of entry into the federal marketplace or a targeted federal agency. Most books are written by authors that work in industry and not in the federal government. I have worked inside of the federal government for 32 years and have institutional knowledge of what can be done by both experienced and inexperience contractors to help increase their prospects of winning a federal government contract. Many of these techniques are not used by the most experienced contractors.

The marketing and sales techniques detailed in this book were documented by collaborating with federal government contractors and federal employees over my career. As a result, I understand the best practices of successful companies. I have also witnessed the worst marketing and sales techniques that have resulted in the turnovers of CEOs or demise of once prominent companies. I have seen small businesses grow into multimillion dollar companies in a very short period of time and can tell you how they did it. As a result of my experience developed over a 32 year federal contracting career, I will provide you with required knowledge, tools, and techniques for success. Being an insider to federal contracting, I was enlightened how contractors became successful. Very few people inside or outside the government get to award and manage government contracts, and talk to the many CEOs, CFOs, and sales staff as I did over my 32 year career. Through these experiences, I have real value to offer to experienced and inexperienced personnel that are eager to obtain government contracts.

The fundamentals of success in federal government contracting are based on three principles. The three principles will always be the keys to success. These three principles are the backbone of the book. The three principles include gaining knowledge, gathering information, and building relationships. These principles are all interdependent upon each other. If you do not develop or have the skills in each of these key areas, you will not be successful in federal contracting. Each principle relies on the other principle. Without the skill of each one of these key principles you will have a difficult time increasing your federal sales. You must be highly skilled in each of these vital areas to increase the probability of success.

GAINING KNOWLEDGE

Before you begin to prepare a proposal for a federal solicitation, you must obtain basic and detailed knowledge. Basic knowledge includes knowing how to properly structure your company, completing the government forms properly, and understanding your product's advantages in the federal marketplace. Your basic knowledge in these areas is critical before you can begin to market and sell to the federal government.

Detailed knowledge includes many aspects of federal contracting. A few key areas include understanding the acquisition rules and regulations and how they may help or hurt your company. Additionally, a company must understand the work being performed at your targeted agency and have a thorough understanding of how the rules and regulations impacts how a targeted agency buys products and services. No one can understand every rule and regulation. However, if you know the general rules and regulations and know where to find the details, you can be successful in the federal marketplace. Throughout this book, I will provide key detailed information that will increase your knowledge to help you win a government contract.

The knowledge of the products and services you are selling to the government and being able to adequately document them in a government technical and business proposal is also a key required skill set. The information required in the preparation of technical and business proposals could be a separate book unto itself and therefore will not be discussed in this book.

Gaining knowledge of your targeted agency is one key component to help you be successful. It often takes federal sales staff years to understand the work that is being performed in a targeted agency. Without this knowledge, you cannot intelligently communicate with federal or contractor contacts about your company and how the company's core competencies match the goals of the agency.

In particular, to be successful you must gain knowledge about federal acquisition strategies that contracting officials use to procure an agency's products and services. Federal agencies often use acquisition techniques to procure products and services in an expeditious manner. You can learn their techniques by accessing various federal databases and/or building relationships with federal and other contractor personnel. Without this knowledge, you may be targeting an agency that uses acquisition techniques that eliminate you from consideration. This is one reason why gaining knowledge is so critical to your success.

Gaining knowledge is one piece of the puzzle you must have to be successful. Throughout the book, I will describe the knowledge you will need and how to obtain the knowledge to be successful.

GATHER INFORMATION

Gathering information is one of the ongoing components to being successful in government contracting. There are a lot of ways to gather information. Your job is to gather as much information as possible so you can make prudent business decisions to help you win a government contract. Information gathering can take place in many forms. It can be found in writing or it can obtained talking to the right person. Information gathering is important and will make the difference in winning a government contract. This book will provide guidelines describing how to gather information, where to gather information, and when to gather it. We will discuss where to find information as well as whom the key players are that will provide you with this information. I will provide sources of information that you were unaware of that are right at your fingertips. I will also explain how successful contractors gather information. Information gathering never ends in federal government contracting. Your organization must establish best practices for gathering information so that you can stay ahead of your competition and develop sound approaches to target the right acquisitions. This book will give you the information gathering techniques to be successful.

BUILD RELATIONSHIPS

A key to any businesses success is developing personal/professional relationships and this is no different in government contracting. Building relationships provides you with real advantages that help your company to be one step ahead of the competition. To be successful in government contracting today, you need to build relationships with both federal officials and contractor personnel. There are differences in terms of how to engage federal staff versus contractor staff. However, in today's marketplace, it is necessary to establish relationships with both federal and contractor staff to be successful.

Federal government contracting offices are run by people like you and me. They have no political party affiliation when they do their jobs. Your job is to establish relationships with these officials so that they develop a level of trust with you and your company. This will go a long way to help you win a government contract. Techniques used to engage federal personnel will be explained in greater detail in subsequent chapters. Almost every business development representative that I have met through the years does not understand how the Federal Acquisition Regulations (FAR) can be applied to help you establish relationships with federal officials.

Government officials are often hard to contact or meet in person. If you currently have government contracts, remember that the government officials are not consciously ignoring your company. They are just very busy purchasing products and services for the government, in the most efficient and effective possible manner. They are always looking ahead to the next acquisition. Their job is to include contractors with the right products and services in the acquisition process. By building relationships, you can help them to become familiar with your company's products and services. That will go a long way to helping you win a government contract.

The federal government regulations encourage you to communicate with federal officials. As a result, the federal regulations help you to build relationships with federal officials. I will provide you with the FAR cite that

7

encourages communication and provides you with the tools and techniques to help you to build the relationships.

Establishing relationships with contractor personnel is just as important as establishing relationships with government personnel. In today's marketplace, two contractors can be teamed together on a proposal today and proposing against each other on another proposal tomorrow and that it perfectly okay. The goal is to win a government contract. Whether you function as a prime, a subcontractor, or work in a joint teaming arrangement, if you can create win-win situations for your company and another company, it is good business. You cannot create the arrangement unless you have developed a professional relationship with the contractor personnel. I am going to explain the steps you can take to make it happen.

This book discusses how to win a federal contract. It is not focused on helping you to win a federal grant. A federal contract is different than a federal grant. The FAR states that a federal contract is an agreement between a buyer (government) and seller (contractor) to furnish supplies and services for a cost/price. Grants.gov states that a federal grant is an award of financial assistance to a recipient to carry out and support a public purpose. This book is not intended to help you win a federal grant, which follows a different set of rules and regulations as compared to contracts. However, it may give you some techniques that will help you in the grants arena.

If you do win a contract with the federal government, it can be an exciting and challenging way to earn a living. You need to know the various complex rules, regulations, processes, and procedures, or know someone who can explain or teach them to you before you can win a government contract. Many contracting officials, government sales staff and corporate CEOs do not know how to play the government contracting game, and do not know how to consistently win contracts. I have met sales staff who have been selling to the federal government for dozens of years and still do not use all of the possible techniques. The government contracting officials are overwhelmed with awarding acquisitions and managing contracts and do not have a lot time to meet with and train unknowledgeable contractors. Therefore, government officials will generally not spend time teaching you how to market and sell to the government.

If you are successful in the federal marketplace, it can also be very profitable for your business. Bette Davis once said, "Getting old isn't for sissies." I could say the same for federal government contracting. You have to be tough, focused, and tenacious to reach your federal government sales goal. Use this book to understand what you need to do to be successful. Once you begin to apply this book's key tools and techniques, you will find your business flourishing.

This book contains many key points and techniques that are not discussed in other training sessions, conferences, or books. To whet your appetite regarding the content of this book, a few techniques that are rarely understood or used by industry personnel that will be discussed in subsequent chapters include the following:

1. Do you know what FAR 15.201 states and how it can be used effectively to win a contract? I have seen contractors win contracts using this clause and I will explain how and why the clause is so important.
2. Do you know how and when it is appropriate to train government staff during a sales meeting to help you win a government contract? It is something that you must do in every meeting and I bet you never do it.

3. Do you know when to ask a government official how your Past Performance evaluation will be conducted? I bet you do it at the wrong time.
4. Do you how the Jumpstart Our Business Startups Act is an advantage to you? If you do not you are missing out on potential opportunities.
5. Do you know the four universal techniques that you must use to secure a meeting with agency staff? The knowledge of these four techniques will give you an advantage in the federal marketplace.
6. Do you know what Federal Data Procurement System is and how to use it? Hopefully you are using it. If you are not using it, you are way behind your competition.

This book is going to deliver proven techniques that are not discussed in other books and are not used by the most experienced contractors. You may already know some of the information and techniques contained in this book; however, I am 100% sure that if you read this book, you will gain insight into additional proven techniques that will give you an advantage in the federal contracting marketplace.

If you want to grow your federal government contracting opportunities, you need to start by developing knowledge and tools for success. In addition, you must develop marketing plans for your company. Follow the tools and techniques in this book, and develop your own marketing plan. Create realistic timelines to make your goal a reality, and do not doubt your path. It is possible to achieve your federal sales and marketing goals as long as you successfully gain knowledge, gather information, and build relationships.

CHAPTER 2

GETTING STARTED – THE BASICS

There are a few basic points you need to know if you want to contract with the federal government. In this Chapter, I will discuss the basic reasons why you may want to contract with the government as well as the basic steps you need to take before you can really get started.

The federal government provides many substantial advantages for contracting as compared to the commercial marketplace. The key reasons why you may want to enter the federal marketplace include the following:

LARGEST BUYER IN THE WORLD

The federal government is the largest buyer of goods and services in the world. USASpending.gov reported that in Fiscal Year 2014, the federal government awarded contracts totaling 443 billion dollars. In addition, the federal government's Small Business Administration sets a goal that approximately 23% of all contracts to small businesses each year. As a result of the federal government's continuous and significant spending on contracts, if you are a business owner, you cannot afford to miss out on federal government contracting opportunities. The federal government will continue to be the largest buyer of goods and services in the world resulting in continuous contracting opportunities for your company.

OPPORTUNITIES ARE PUBLICIZED

One of the advantages of contracting with the federal government is that it offers thousands of opportunities each year. Many of these opportunities are posted on the government's Federal Business Opportunities (FedBizOpps) website, https://www.fbo.gov/. This website is available to the public including federal contractors. This website also posts "Award Notices" and "Sources Sought" information. The government regulations require that opportunities posted in FedBizOpps be open for at least thirty days to allow adequate time for vendors to prepare and submit proposals. This location helps to level the playing field for all federal contractors by allowing all vendors to view what the government is buying. All eligible vendors have the same opportunity to view the website, review the government requirements, and submit a proposal.

LONG TERM CONTRACTS

Another reason to sell to the federal government is the length of performance of most contracts; many federal government contracts last for five years or more. That means that sales are locked up for that time period. For example, the Coast Guard, for example, awarded a contract a few years ago that called for a twenty-five year period of performance. This long term commitment is a big deal for any company. Depending on the size of the company and the contract type, the government may also pay an allocated portion of your direct and indirect expenses during the life of the contract. Long term contracts offer security for both the company and its employees.

FAST PAYMENT

The federal government procures a large variety of products and services each year, and needs a large array of contractors to meet the delivery demands. It also maintains a strict payment schedule, and pays its contractors promptly. The FAR requires payment to federal contractors be made within thirty days of receipt of an invoice for most contractors and fifteen days for small businesses contractors. This fast payment separates the U.S. government from the private and commercial marketplace, where commercial clients often hold money for a longer period of time, if they pay at all. If the U.S. government does not pay you within the specified days noted in the contract, federal law dictates that it must pay your company interest on the money it owes. As a result of this law, the government almost always pays on time. This is advantageous for companies both large and small as they seek to balance their budgets and control cash flow. It also provides companies with the peace-of-mind to know that they will be promptly paid for their products and/or services.

CREDIT CARDS

The U.S. government buys a lot of products using government credit cards, referred to in the government as "purchase cards." In accordance with the FAR, a large number of employees have been granted the authority to use credit/purchase cards for smaller purchases up to $3,000. The employees using the purchase cards are not necessarily contracting officers and contracting specialists. The employees with the limited purchase card authority are spread throughout all of the offices and organizations in an agency. If you can engage the appropriate federal officials, you can take advantage of their ability to use credit cards to increase your sales. This is a streamlined process that allows the federal government to buy its products and services in an efficient and effective manner. If you can learn how to tap into the purchase card process, it can result in substantial sales for your company. Purchase cards can also be used to place a task or delivery order if authorized in the basic contract, basic ordering agreement, or blanket purchase agreement, and can also be used to make payments when the contractor agrees to accept payment by the purchase card.

COST REIMBURSEMENT CONTRACTS

Another advantage to contracting with the federal government is that you can submit proposals for the most advantageous solicitations. Solicitations for government cost reimbursement contracts are terrific for small and large companies since it places most of the performance risk on the government. The government is also only required to reimburse the company for its best efforts. Cost reimbursement contracts are very advantageous to large or small businesses because the government will pay your indirect costs if they are fair and reasonable, allowable in accordance with the regulations and allocable to the work on the government contract. These types of contracts are very beneficial to any government contractor and are not often used in the commercial marketplace.

SMALL BUSINESS ADVANTAGES

Small businesses have particular advantages in the federal acquisition process. All federal agencies are required to award a certain percentage of contracts to small businesses. According to the SBA, that percentage has recently been as high as 23% of total contract dollars awarded government wide. This means that the government officials must find small businesses to deliver substantial amounts of supplies and perform the services needed by an agency. These small business goals are usually part of an agency's yearly performance goals and the government senior official's performance goals. If the federal agencies do not reach their goals, it can impact the performance evaluations of the senior officials. Therefore, agencies do all that they can to achieve these small business goals.

14

The U.S. government acquisition rules and regulations, as shown in the FAR, are advantageous to small businesses. All acquisitions below the simplified acquisition threshold ($150,000 in 2014) are set-aside for small businesses. For acquisitions over the simplified threshold, federal contracting officials must meet with federal small business officials before they can issue solicitations, to determine if the products and services must be "set-aside" for small business. In accordance with the FAR, if they are below $4,000,000, certain classes of small business acquisitions can be awarded on a noncompetitive basis. The government officials like awarding small business contracts because there are streamlined acquisition processes for small business awards below certain dollar thresholds. Therefore, it is often faster and easier for federal agency personnel to award contracts to small businesses. I will go into detail of the small business advantages in Chapter 3.

The U.S. government assigns thousands of employees, titled "Small Business Specialists" or "Small Business Professionals" to federal agencies just to aid small businesses. If you are a small business, this means that you have federal personnel available to help you win a contract. The small business specialists will be your advocate to helping you find opportunities at an agency. They will help you to maneuver through the rules and regulations and assist you in learning how an agency functions. They may also reveal specific agency opportunities that will match your skill sets. The federal government places these personnel in each agency to help you to be successful, which is a big advantage to any small business.

RESTRICTIONS

If you are currently a federal employee or are forming a business with a federal employee because of their knowledge, you need to stop immediately. Federal contracting officials cannot enter into contracts with an active federal employee. The FAR Part 3.601 states that:

> A contracting officer shall not knowingly award a contract to a Government employee or to a business concern or other organization owned or substantially owned or controlled by one or more Government employees. This policy is intended to avoid any conflict of interest that might arise between the employees' interests and their Government duties and to avoid the appearance of favoritism or preferential treatment by the Government toward its employees.

Therefore, do not go down the path of entering into a business relationship with a federal employee unless they are retired and/or have received clearance by their agency's ethics office.

Once you consider the advantages of contracting with the government and decide to move forward, you need to take a few initial steps to properly organize and structure your company. These initial steps are important in terms of how they may impact your ability to receive government contracts in the future.

CORPORATE STRUCTURE

The federal government acquisition rules are very advantageous to certain classes of businesses. Therefore, before you can market your company to the government, you need to think about how to structure it in accordance with those rules. The correct structure provides companies distinct advantages in the federal government marketplace. On the other hand, incorrect structuring may create a huge disadvantage in your ability to win government contracts. For example, if you structure your company as a certain class of a small disadvantaged business, the Federal Acquisition Regulation authorizes you to receive noncompetitive contract awards up to $4,000,000 (FAR).

If you form a non-profit organization to compete for federal grants and contracts, you will be at a severe disadvantage for receiving contracts because of your non-profit status. That is because all non-profit organizations are considered large businesses in the federal contracting arena. They cannot be considered small businesses in federal contracting because they receive distinct tax advantages as compared to commercial organizations. If you have a non-profit organization with five personnel, you are considered a large business in the federal contracting. Therefore, non-profit organizations have a tougher time competing in the federal contracting marketplace.

In addition, if you are non-profit organization and you want to subcontract with other federal government contractors, they may not want to contract with you. Why? Just like the government agencies, government contractors also have small business contracting goals that they need to achieve in each government contract. These goals are similar to each federal agency's small business contracting goals. Non-profit organizations do not contribute to the federal government's or contractor's small business contracting goals. A contractor may not be selected for a prime contract or subcontract award if they cannot demonstrate that they can achieve the targeted small business subcontracting goals.

According to the Small Business Administration, before you can sell to the federal government, you need to have your company's business in order. Your business must be financially stable and there must be a demand for your product or service. It also must have staff devoted to the federal marketplace and have a corporate pricing structure competitive in your industry. Finally, there must be a proven sales history of your products and services. Government officials may come to your business location to ensure that you are a real contractor and have a record of selling your product.

Businesses are afforded unique opportunities in federal contracting if they are structured properly. You need to structure your corporation correctly to increase your chance of success in the federal marketplace. Chapter 3 will discuss how your company can be structured to take advantage of federal government small business rules and regulations.

OBTAIN A LOCAL BUSINESS LICENSE

Once you have chosen the structure for your business, you need to register with your state and/or local government for a business license. Contact your state and/or local government representative to determine how and where to register your business. These processes vary from state to state. Ask your state and/or local representative about any other applications, permits, and/or licenses that are required to conduct business in the state or city.

OBTAIN A TAX IDENTIFICATION NUMBER

Once you have structured your business and obtained the appropriate business license(s), the next step is to obtain a tax identification number. The Tax ID number is called the Federal Employer Identification Number, referred to as the Federal EIN; this is obtained through the Internal Revenue Service (IRS). The Federal EIN can be obtained quickly by calling 1-800-829-4933 (from 7:00 a.m. until 10:00 p.m.) or through the IRS website at http://www.irs.gov/Businesses/Small-Businesses-&-Self-Employed/Apply-for-an-Employer-Identification-Number-(EIN)-Online. You will have to complete a SS-4 form during the process. You can find the SS-4 form and its instructions on the IRS website.

OBTAIN A DATA UNIVERSAL NUMBERING SYSTEM NUMBER

Obtaining a Data Universal Numbering System (DUNS) number is a mandatory requirement for bidding on government work. It is provided for free by Dun and Bradstreet, a private Wall Street corporation. The website is http://www.dnb.com/. A DUNS number is a universally recognized standard number used to identify and track businesses worldwide. A DUNS number provides a business with credibility in the marketplace because people who want to know facts about any business can go to the DUNS website and read a company's profile.

NORTH AMERICAN INDUSTRIAL CLASSIFICATION SYSTEM (NAICS) CODES AND SIZE STANDARDS

The government needs to verify whether you are classified as a large or small business before you can begin to receive government contracts. You will have to determine your size standard before you can propose on a government contract. The government sets the size standards on an industry-by-industry basis, depending on the type of work your business performs. The size standards are applied using the industry definitions found in the North American Industry Classification System (NAICS) Manual available via the internet at:

www.census.gov/epcd/www/naics.html.

The FAR Part 19.102 "Size Standards" states:

(a) The SBA establishes small business size standards on an industry-by-industry basis. (See 13 CFR Part 121.)

(b) Small business size standards are applied by—

(1) Classifying the product or service being acquired in the industry whose definition, as found in the North American Industry Classification System (NAICS) Manual (available on the Internet at: www.census.gov/epcd/www/naics.html, best describes the principal nature of the product or service being acquired;

(2) Identifying the size standard SBA established for that industry; and

(3) Specifying the size standard in the solicitation so that offerors can appropriately represent themselves as small or large.

If you want to classify your business as a small business in future solicitations, review the NAICS manual size standards, determine which industries your company falls under, and identify the SBA size standard for your company. The NAICS manual helps you find the industry NAICS codes for your products or services, and identifies the SBA-established size standards for that industry. This is the same NAICS manual that helps the government officials establish size standards for their acquisitions. Since it is the government's policy to provide maximum practicable contracting and subcontracting opportunities to small businesses, it is to your advantage to qualify in as many NAICS codes as possible. Determine the proper NAICS codes for your business and use the codes appropriately to maximize your government contracting opportunities.

Once you know your NAICS codes and size standards, you will review each government solicitation and determine if it includes your NAICS codes. The government contracting officer will note the NAICS code and if it is a small business set-aside solicitation. If it is set-aside for small businesses, the NAICS size standards will determine if you can submit a proposal for a particular solicitation. You self-certify your size standard to the contracting officer when you submit a proposal to the government. Nothing else is required.

The SBA is an excellent resource for selecting the appropriate NAICS codes, as they want to provide your business with an opportunity to grow. Contact the SBA with questions and concerns during the selection process. Keep in mind that these standards may change over time and require recertification. The Department of Commerce determines size standards on an annual basis.

The government contracting officer must accept your small business representation for a specific bid or proposal, unless another party challenges your representation or the contracting officer has reason to question the representation. If this happens, the government contracting official refers the challenge to the SBA.

The SBA must review applications for certain small business categories. If you want to become certified as an 8(A) small business or HUBZone small business, you must obtain written certification from the SBA before you can receive an award resulting from a solicitation. For other set-aside designations, an organization may self-certify their small business status or have a third party certify their status.

SYSTEM FOR AWARD MANAGEMENT

Prior to proposing on any government contract, information regarding your company must be registered and entered into a government database. In 2012, the federal government consolidated all of its contract registration sites into one system. The System for Award Management (SAM) is now the official U.S. government system that consolidated the capabilities of the Central Contractor Registration, Online Representations, and Certifications Application (ORCA), and the Excluded Parties List System (EPLS).

Prior to proposing on a government solicitation, you must register in the SAM database. The registration website is SAM.gov. The SAM is the primary vendor database for the federal government. The SAM collects, validates, stores, and disseminates data for federal contracting officials. Both current and potential government vendors must register in the SAM in order to receive federal contract awards or extensions. This one-time registration provides some basic company information, including financial information, and must be renewed annually.

Your registration in the SAM also authorizes the government to pay you electronically, provides your company a Commercial and Government Entity (CAGE) code and a Marketing Partner ID number. Being registered in the SAM also grants you access to other Government applications, including the government past performance database, which is the official report card of company's performance on past government contracts.

Federal contracting officials must review certain aspects of your business each time you submit a proposal. Prior to January 2005, companies were required to complete and submit Representation and Certification forms with every proposal. After January 2005, the FAR was changed to mandate that all prospective contractors complete the forms in the SAM. To adequately complete the SAM process, you must fill out certain forms found in an area of the SAM database called "Review Rep and Certs." The "Review Rep and Certs" section of the SAM streamlines the representation and certification process for both the contractor and government officials, and is a part of Section K of the government solicitation document.

The information in the "Review Rep and Certs" helps the government maintain a current contractor information database. The SAM should be updated if the information contained in it changes. Most companies update the information annually. Some contracts require specific representations and certifications outside of the electronic SAM "Review Rep and Certs" process and provide these additional documents in the solicitation. The advantage of the SAM "Review Rep and Certs" section is that the government officials now have one repository for vendor certifications. The information generated from the "Review Rep and Certs" section of the SAM is easily reproduced by government representatives to become a part of the official government contract award file. It is important to verify the information in this section is up-to-date prior to submitting a proposal for a government solicitation.

Once you have completed the certification in the "Review Rep and Certs" section of the SAM, along with the other forms and certifications described above, you have completed the registration process. That is the easy part. Winning a government contract is the hard part. However, if you have made it this far, you have the guts and determination necessary to successfully win government contracts.

FINAL POINT: RULES AND REGULATIONS

The federal contracting rules and regulations are very complex. Each contract document contains a lot of rules and regulations. The federal government contracting officials follow federal government rules and regulations. The rules and regulations are contained in the Federal Acquisition Regulation, otherwise referred to as the FAR, which can be found at https://www.acquisition.gov/Far/. The FAR contains fifty-three different subparts which are all used in various aspects of federal contracting. The FAR provides important guidelines for contracting with the federal government.

Individual agencies have their own regulations that provide additional details that supplement the FAR. For instance, the Department of Defense has the Defense Federal Acquisition Regulation Supplement (DFAR), while the Department of Health and Human Services has the Health and Human Services Acquisition Regulation (HHSAR) supplement. The DFAR can be found at: http://www.acq.osd.mil/dpap/dars/dfarspgi/current/ and the HHSAR can be found at: http://www.hhs.gov/policies/hhsar/. Agency supplements do not replace or trump the language contained in the FAR. These supplemental regulations provide additional agency instructions regarding how to implement the FAR.

In addition to the FAR websites, the government has placed all of the key acquisition information into one website at http://www.acquisition.gov. This website contains links to important federal websites described throughout this book. If you are or want to become a federal contractor, I would recommend saving this website link on your computer.

As a result of the complexity of the federal government acquisition rules and regulations, your organization must at a minimum have personnel that know what is included in and where to find information contained in the FAR. There are too many federal contracting rules and regulations for any one person to know. However, you need personnel with familiarity of the FAR and other federal acquisition rules and regulations to be a successful government contractor.

CHAPTER 3

SMALL BUSINESS ADVANTAGES

According to the Small Business Administration (SBA), in Fiscal Year 2013, the federal government awarded over 83.1 billion dollars in government contracts to small businesses. It also reported that 23.39% of all government contract award dollars went to small businesses. This is really good news if you are a small business. Small businesses have large advantages when contracting with the federal government. In this chapter, I will examine the advantages of contracting as a small business and how the rules and regulations benefit your company. Once you know the small business rules and regulations, you will increase your chances of winning a government contract.

The SBA Act is implemented by regulations that are published in the Federal Register prior to finalization. Anyone can provide input to the Federal Register notice prior to the finalization of the regulations. The SBA's regulations are found in the Code of Federal Regulations (CFR), Title 13, Business Credit and Assistance, Chapters 1 - 199. The CFR is the codification of the general and permanent rules published in the Federal Register by the executive departments and agencies of the federal government. It is divided into fifty titles that represent broad areas. Each volume of the CFR is updated once each year and is issued on a quarterly basis.

The FAR Part 19, Small Business Programs, implements the information contained in the CFR regulations, Title 13, Business Credit and Assistance, Chapters 1 - 199. The FAR does not contain every regulation that is found in the CFR, so if you want to know the SBA rules and regulations, read the CFR. If you want to understand the more general information that government contracting officials use to award contracts to small businesses, read the FAR Part 19.

The definition of a small business is contained in the CFR. Title 13, Business Credit and Assistance, Chapters 1 - 199. The SBA website defines a small business as an organization that must be independently owned and operated for profit, is not dominant in its particular field, and is qualified under the SBA's size standards in terms of the number of employees and annual sales. The size standards are found in the Title 13, Chapter 121 of the CFR.

The federal government has small business contracting goals for each fiscal year. The goals are established by Congress and are found in the SBA Act. The small business goals as were stated in the SBA Act in Fiscal Year 2015 were as follows:

Government-wide Small Business: The government-wide goal for participation by small business concerns is 23 percent of the total value of all prime contract awards.

Small business concerns owned and controlled by socially and economically disadvantaged individuals: 5% of all prime contract and subcontract awards for the fiscal year.

Women-Owned Small Business: 5% of all prime contract and subcontract awards for the fiscal year.

HUB Zone Small Business: 3% of all prime contract and subcontract awards for the fiscal year.

Service-Disabled Veteran-Owned Small Business: 3% of all prime contract and subcontract awards for the fiscal year.

Individual federal agencies have small business goals that may vary slightly from the government-wide goals. These variations are due to an agency's unique circumstance(s) that may impact their ability to meet the government-wide goal. In order to meet their small business goals, agencies set-aside a certain portion of their acquisitions for small businesses. The SBA Set-Aside Program allows agencies to award certain acquisitions exclusively to small business concerns. Only a set-aside small business can bid/propose on these acquisitions. A small business set-aside solicitation may only be offered to certain types of small or small disadvantaged businesses.

In federal government contracting, there are two general types of small businesses. There are Small Businesses and Small Disadvantaged Businesses. The term Small Business represents all of the small businesses in the federal marketplace. It includes all classes of small businesses. Small Disadvantaged Businesses represent certain classes of small businesses that are afforded unique opportunities to propose on federal contracts because of their "disadvantaged" status.

SMALL BUSINESS

As is noted in the FAR Part 19, if you are a small business, the SBA allows contractors to self-certify their small business size status. This reduces the paperwork for the SBA, and makes it easier for contractors to bid on government contracts and subcontracts. Only certified small businesses can propose on small business set-aside solicitations. As a result, there is a limited eligible pool of bidders. In addition, all contract awards below the micro-purchase threshold ($150,000 in Fiscal Year 2015) must be awarded to small businesses.

The prime advantage of being a self-certified small business is the ability to propose on the same solicitations as large businesses. However, large businesses cannot bid on the solicitations exclusively reserved by the government for small businesses. If you are a new company, it's a good idea to concentrate on the federal small business opportunities. Do not waste your time and resources competing with the large businesses unless you are relatively sure you will win. Increase your odds by proposing on the federal small business opportunities where you will have less competition, which will increase your chance of winning a federal contract.

Most solicitations set-aside for small businesses will be publicized on the Federal Business Opportunities website. Some small business opportunities are not publicized. The rationale to publicize or not publicize is based on the dollar thresholds established in the FAR. Small Business opportunities must be posted on the Federal Business Opportunities website unless it is an exception noted in FAR Subpart 5.202 "Exceptions." In general, small business solicitations do not have to be published if they are below dollar thresholds established by the SBA for certain classes of small business set-asides. Most of the small business solicitations that are not publicized are for Small Disadvantaged Business concern companies.

SMALL DISADVANTAGED BUSINESS CONCERN

If you are considered a Small Disadvantaged Business (SDB) concern company, you will have additional advantages in federal contracting. To qualify as a SDB concern, the SBA requires that your company must be at least 51% owned, operated and managed on a daily basis by one or more socially and economically disadvantaged individuals, and be a small business according to SBA's size standards. Federal agencies are required by the SBA to set aside a certain number of acquisitions for SDBs. Since October 2008, small businesses can self-represent their status as a SDB. You do not have to submit an application to the SBA to receive a SDB certification. However, you must understand the SBA eligibility criteria for SDBs. A SDB self-certifies that it is a SDB concern. The self-certification may be protested by another contractor during the competitive bidding process.

If an acquisition has been determined to be a SDB Set-Aside by the federal government, it means that it is reserved exclusively for SDBs. This limits the number of contractors proposing on the work. The government intentionally wants to give small businesses opportunities to succeed by limiting the number of companies that can bid on set-aside solicitations. Solicitations below certain dollar thresholds do not have to be published and the awards can be made on a non-competitive basis.

There are four categories of SDBs defined in the FAR that offer distinct advantages in federal contracting as compared to a regular small business. These SDB concerns include:

1. The Service-Disabled Veteran-Owned Small Business Program
2. The Historically Underutilized Business Zone (HUBZONE) Program
3. The Women-Owned Small Business Concerns Program
4. The 8(a) Business Development Program

SERVICE-DISABLED VETERAN-OWNED SMALL BUSINESS PROGRAM

The Service-Disabled Veteran-Owned Small Business Program is a relatively new Small Disadvantaged Business

31

Program. Service-Disabled Veteran-Owned contractors can now be set-aside and competed only amongst other Service-Disabled Veteran-Owned Small Businesses. As of Fiscal Year 2015, the FAR states that this type of set-aside business can receive non-competitive contract awards up to $3,500,000 for service and construction acquisitions and $6,000,000 for manufacturing acquisitions if no other Service-Disabled Veteran-Owned contractors are known to exist for a similar product or service. If other Service-Disabled Veteran-Owned Small Businesses exist, the acquisition must be competed among all Service-Disabled Veteran-Owned Small Businesses.

A Service-Disabled Veteran-Owned Small Business must qualify as a small business under the criteria and size standards in the 13th Code of Federal Regulations (CFR) 125.8-125.10. According to the CFR, this set-aside type must be at least 51% unconditionally owned, operated, and managed on a daily basis by a service disabled veteran who demonstrates a potential for success. A service disabled veteran must only be 1% disabled to qualify for this program. The SBA does not certify the disability of the veteran. The Veterans Administration must verify and certify this information. The spouse of a service disabled veteran with a permanent or severe disability or their permanent caregiver can also qualify for this program. This is a fast growing set-aside category of the SBA Small Disadvantaged Business Program.

HISTORICALLY UNDERUTILIZED BUSINESS ZONE PROGRAM

The Historically Underutilized Business Zone (HUBZone) Program authorizes set-aside preferences to federal procurement opportunities for small businesses in urban and rural communities. The set-aside preferences are available to small businesses that obtain HUBZone certifications from the SBA in part by employing staff who live in the SBA designated HUBZone areas. The main contractor's office must be located within a designated HUBZone area, and at least 35% of the employees must reside in a HUBZone area. The map of the HUBZone designated areas can be found on the SBA's website. The HUBZone criteria and size standards are found in 13th CFR 121. In addition, the business must be at least 51% unconditionally owned, operated, and managed on a daily basis by a U.S. citizen. The SBA initiated the HUBZone Program to stimulate economic development and create jobs in urban and rural communities. As of Fiscal Year 2015, the FAR Part 19 states that HUBZone contractors can receive contracts up to $4,000,000 in value under certain circumstances on a non-competitive basis for service and construction acquisitions and $6,500,000 for manufacturing acquisitions, if no other HUBZone contractors are known to exist for a similar product or service. Otherwise, the acquisition must be competed among other HUBZone contractors.

WOMEN-OWNED SMALL BUSINESS CONCERN PROGRAM

The Women-Owned Small Business Concern and/or Economically Disadvantaged Women-Owned Small Business Concern contractor must qualify as a small business under the criteria and size standards in the 13th CFR 121. A federal agency may set-aside a contract for Economically Disadvantaged Women-Owned Small Business Concerns and Women-Owned Small Business Concerns if the North American Industry Classification System (NAICS) code for the contract is underrepresented by Women-Owned Small Business Concerns. NAICS information is used by federal agencies in classifying businesses so that data can be collected, analyzed, and published. If the NAICS code used on a contract is underrepresented for Women-Owned businesses, the requirement can be set-aside and competed amongst other Women-Owned Small Business Concerns or Economically Disadvantaged Women-Owned Small Business Concerns. You can find the underrepresented NAICS codes on the SBA's website.

Women-Owned Small Business Concerns must be at least 51% unconditionally owned, operated, and managed on a daily basis by one or more women. The contracting officials can only utilize this program if there is a reasonable expectation that two or more proposals will be received. However, if only one proposal is received, the award can still be made. There are no dollar limit thresholds for Women-Owned Small Business Concerns.

However, in December 2014, the U.S. Congress passed a law that fundamentally changed the Women-Owned Small Business Concerns Program. Under the National Defense Authorization Act (NDAA) for fiscal year 2015, contracting officers can now award, when appropriate, sole source contracts to eligible Women-Owned Small Businesses. This new law creates parity between the Women-Owned Small Business Concerns Program and other small and disadvantaged business programs. More contracting dollars will be awarded to Women-Owned Small Business Concerns in the near future. The law eliminated the self-certification requirement and will require the SBA to create its own certification process. It will take a period of time for this new law to be promulgated in the FAR. Stay tuned and keep informed of these future changes to the FAR.

8(a) BUSINESS DEVELOPMENT PROGRAM

The 8(a) Business Development Program differs from the Small Disadvantaged Business Program in that the

SBA must certify if a contractor qualifies as an 8(a) designated contractor. The 8(a) Business Development Program is described in the 13th CFR 121. To qualify as an 8(a) Business Development Program contractor, the company must be at least 51% unconditionally owned, operated, and managed on a daily basis by one or more socially and economically disadvantaged U.S. citizens, who must demonstrate a potential for success. Socially and economically disadvantaged U.S. citizens include Black Americans, Hispanic Americans, Native Americans (American Indians, Eskimos, Aleuts, and Native Hawaiians), and Asian Pacific Americans. As of Fiscal Year 2015, the FAR states that 8(a) Business Development Program contractors can receive contracts up to $4,000,000 on a non-competitive basis for service or construction acquisitions and $6,500,000 for manufacturing acquisitions. If the acquisition is over the non-competitive thresholds, it must be competed among 8(a) contractors. Contractors must submit an 8(a) certification form to the SBA to qualify for this program. Contractors must receive the certification from the SBA before they can begin to propose on federal contracts as a certified 8(a) contractor.

The 8(a) Business Development Program is the most advantageous SBA set-aside program in federal contracting because you can receive non-competitive awards. It is fairly easy to qualify, if according to the SBA, you have been in business for two years and 51% of your business is owned and managed by a socially and economically disadvantaged U.S. citizen. 8(a) companies can also form Joint Ventures with other businesses to help them compete on government contracts. I will go into detail about Joint Ventures in a later chapter.

35

8(a) companies can also be accepted into the 8(a) Mentor Protégé Program. This Program will allow successful businesses to team with a new or small 8(a) company to teach it how to be successful in the federal marketplace. I will discuss the 8(a) Mentor Protégé Program in a later chapter. The 8(a) Program has a lot of advantages in government contracting.

The SBA website lists the following requirements to become certified as an 8(a) contractor:

• The business must be majority-owned (51% or more) by an individual(s).

• The individual(s) must be an American citizen, by birth or naturalization.

• The business must be majority-owned (51% or more) and controlled/managed by socially and economically disadvantaged individual(s).

• The individual(s) controlling and managing the firm on a full-time basis must meet the SBA requirement for disadvantage, by proving both social disadvantage and economic disadvantage.

• The business must be a small business.

•The business must demonstrate potential for success.

• The principals must show good character.

ACQUISITIONS LESS THAN $3,000 AND LESS THAN $150,000

According to the FAR, acquisitions less than $3,000 do not have to be awarded to small business entities. They can be awarded to small or large contractors. In addition, competition is not required because the government wants to award these small actions in an efficient and effective manner. If actions below $3,000 were competed, the government would spend more than $3,000 in labor resources to procure the products or services.

As is shown in the FAR, acquisitions greater than $3,000 and less than $150,000 are reserved exclusively for small businesses (see FAR 19.502-2). For acquisitions less than $150,000, contracting officials have the discretion to make the award to any type of small business, including any type of small business set-aside. If you are a small business, winning numerous acquisitions less than $150,000 can quickly accumulate significant increases in overall sales. However, you have to look for and find these acquisition and bid on them to be successful.

ADVANTAGES AND DISADVANTAGES OF THE SET-ASIDE PROGRAMS

The SBA set-aside program has changed significantly over the past twenty years. In the 1980s and 1990s, only 8(a) and HUBZone contractors received awards as a Small Disadvantaged Business Concern. There was a limited pool of contractors that were receiving set-aside federal contract awards. With the recent changes in set-aside procedures for Service-Disabled Veteran-Owned Small Business Concerns, Economically Disadvantaged Women-Owned Small Business Concerns, and Women-Owned Small Business Concerns, more contractors are now able to compete as a Small Disadvantaged Business Concern. This is really good news if you are a Service-Disabled Veteran-Owned Small Business or Women-Owned Small Business and bad news if you are an existing 8(a) or HUBZone contractor. Federal agencies now have more set-aside categories to choose from when developing acquisition strategies.

Although federal agencies now have more set-aside categories for acquisitions, recurring 8(a) contracting requirements must remain in the existing 8(a) program.

This means that once a requirement is placed in the 8(a) program, it must remain in that set-aside category unless the requirement significantly changes or contractors cannot be found in that category. Only new requirements can be considered for one of the four SDB categories. Many new contractors are being certified into these SDB categories and competing for the work. As a result of the recent changes in the regulations, a lot of new Service-Disabled Veteran-Owned and Women-Owned businesses will be competing for work that would have previously been placed in the 8(a) or HUBZone programs. With the additional set-aside categories, more contractors will try to influence federal officials to place new acquisitions in their SDB category.

The SBA does not prevent contractors from qualifying in more than one of the SDB set-aside programs. Therefore, if you are certified by the SBA as an 8(a) contractor, you can also be certified/self-certify as a Service-Disabled Veteran-Owned contractor, and/or a Women-Owned contractor, and/or a HUBZone contractor. For example, a properly certified African American service-disabled veteran female located in a HUBZone, has the potential to propose on almost all of an agency's set-aside solicitations.

These programs also have disadvantages for contractors in the federal marketplace. Once a federal agency's requirement/contract is placed in one of these four SDB Programs, it is generally only removed from the particular SDB Program if the requirement changes or if there are no other contractors in the particular set-aside category to perform the work. Therefore, if a contract is currently in the 8(a) Business Development Program and your small business is a Service-Disabled Veteran-Owned Small Business, you cannot propose on that solicitation in

38

the future. You always need to know how an agency contracts were previously awarded to determine if you can propose on the requirement in the future. You do not want to waste your company's resources chasing after acquisitions that are unavailable to your small business. This step should be a standard part of your research process, as it will save you both time and money.

SUBCONTRACTS

Government prime contracts awarded to large businesses are required to meet small business goals for subcontracted work. The prime contractor subcontracting goals are similar to federal agency's goals. For example, like federal agencies, 23% of all subcontracted dollars on each large business prime contract should be awarded to small businesses. If you are certified in one of the SDB, both government agencies and government contractors will need you to help them meet their small business goals. Therefore, it will be easier for your company to hunt for government contracts and subcontracts if you are a small business or a SDB.

NONCOMPETITIVE AWARDS FOR CERTAIN DOLLAR THRESHOLDS

The greatest advantage of the SBA's SDB Program is that you can receive multimillion dollar federal awards on a non-competitive basis. You must structure your business accordingly to do so. When you form your Limited Liability Corporation or Sole Proprietor Corporation, you need to make sure that 51% of your business is owned by someone who can give your business a SDB Program set-aside designation. This corporate structure will present the best opportunity to win a government contract. This decision is one of the most important factors to consider in federal government contracting. Do not overlook this point if you are just starting a business or are currently in business. If you want to win an award of a government contract, the SBA's SDB Program is a major technique that must be used to bust into the federal marketplace.

If you are a small business or a small disadvantaged business, you have some real advantages in federal contracting. It will not be easy to win a federal contract, but it will help you to get a foot in the door if you are a properly certified small business. It is important to take advantage of the government rules and regulations if they provide you an opportunity to be successful.

CHAPTER 4

STARTING THE MARKETING & SALES PROCESS

WHAT AM I SELLING TO A TARGETED AGENCY?

What are you selling to the government? To most of us, this seems like an obvious and straightforward question. However, it can get more complicated than you think. Before you walk into a government office to sell your company's products and services, you must have a thorough understanding of them. You must also pinpoint the product or service that you want to sell to the government agency you are targeting, and then you must begin your marketing strategy.

There are many reasons to think about this beforehand. Consider for example, a commercial business with hundreds of thousands and perhaps hundreds of millions of dollars in sales. On the commercial side, the company is successful, and may have many subsidiaries and even name brands that are not sold to the government. Their salesperson may therefore go to the government office and meet with the government contracting and/or program staff in an attempt to sell these products and services by marketing the company. The salesperson may be dressed in an expensive suit, with a professional, glossy sales brochure. That is really good right?

The truth is that it is not good. In reality, the salesperson and the company described had no idea what were the government agency's needs. It happens time-and-time again. Salespersons often have no idea what they

41

should be selling to the government, or what will bring a successful sale. They are in effect, selling the company rather than a specific product. They are also wasting their time as well as the government official's time trying to complete a sale.

Through my years in government contracting, I have seen many presentations from sales staff that were extremely successful in the commercial market, but knew almost nothing about selling their products and services to the government. They came into the government offices thinking that the government officials were going to open their checkbooks and start buying their products or services as soon as they saw the company brochure. That may work in the commercial world, but it is not how the government procurement process works. Federal government contracting is totally different than the commercial marketplace.

Selling to the government must always start with research. Find out what the government needs and decide whether you can satisfy that need. Government officials do not allow salespersons and/or companies to solicit their offices. Therefore, your job is to determine which of your company's products or services are best suited to sell to a particular federal agency.

MEETING WITH FEDERAL OFFICIALS

Why does not the government allow contractors access to its offices? If it did, the government contracting offices would be inundated with contractors trying to sell their products and services. Government officials do not want or need hundreds of sales staff running through the halls. That would just make the government more inefficient and ineffective. Government officials compromise by allowing company personnel to come into the offices on official business. Official business generally means that the industry personnel are meeting with Federal officials on current contracts, or are marketing the latest technology, new products and/or unique services in their industry.

If you have a good idea of what you are selling and know whether the government needs it, you have a better chance of securing a meeting with government officials. If you know your marketing pitch for an individual product or service ahead of time, you will also have a better chance of a successful meeting. Knowing your product and sales pitch means that you can quickly hone in on the purpose of the meeting, with a short one to four minute presentation, and then expand on the advantages of your product. You can finalize a successful meeting by describing why government officials need your product or service.

In the past ten years, the number of federal contracting staff has been drastically reduced. Those that are left do not have the time to meet with everyone who walks into their office. Government officials do not want to meet with anyone unless that person has something of value to bring to the table. A sales brochure has little value in federal contracting. They take up space in federal offices and provide little value regarding what the government officials want and/or need when you meet with them. Contractor business cards provide a little more value, but still do not sell the product or service. As a result of staffing shortages, it will be difficult to meet with contracting officials unless you have done your homework and provide a presentation that has value for the federal contracting officials. I will describe how to do provide value at a meeting with federal officials in Chapter 12.

YOUR FIRST CONTRACT AWARD

The first contract award with the government or a particular targeted federal agency will be the most difficult.

If you target your efforts and know exactly what it is that you want to sell, the second contract award will be easier. You will gain a lot of experience and knowledge securing your first contract award. You will learn how a given federal agency buys their products and services. Once you have figured out the process, the agency or government contractor (if you are a subcontractor) may choose to work with you again and again. Do not get discouraged by the effort it takes you to receive your first contract award. Consider your experience to be part of your learning curve, and persevere through any hurdles you may find to win your first award.

BRANDING THE COMPANY

Once you get that first and second contract award, your company's brand name will become more familiar to the government personnel at an agency. The most effective way to positively brand your company on the first or second award at an agency is to perform in an outstanding manner. You want people to know your company because of the outstanding job you performed on your first contract. This is the best way to help increase your chances of winning future contracts at your targeted agency.

If you do not perform in an outstanding manner on your first or second contract award at a targeted agency, you may never receive another award at that agency because your company's brand name is tarnished. If you do receive a second award after performing poorly, it will take a lot of work to win subsequent awards due to your missteps. The government officials may have been partially at fault, however, that does not matter in this case. Poor performance on your first and second contract is a very damaging outcome, which will impact your chance of success in the federal marketplace.

44

CALCULATE YOUR STEPS

Take the process of marketing and selling slow, with one product or service at a time. The processes and techniques that you use may differ depending on the product or service and how the government buys that particular product or service. Focus on a particular product or service that you know a particular agency needs. Work hard selling that particular product or service to achieve your goal.

If you have a vast array of products and services to sell to the government, but do not know where to start, you will not know how to design the marketing plan. Decide on your product and the agency, and then design the marketing plan around how that agency procures its products and services.

Before you start, make sure that you have selected the appropriate NAICS codes for your business. Failure to do so may result in a restriction from proposing on efforts that are within your corporate capabilities. The Federal Small Business Specialists also use the NAICS codes, which are registered in the SAM to help locate companies with particular products or services. You must know what you are selling to register the products and services appropriately in the SAM.

DEFINING SUCCESS

If you can specifically define the products and services you want to market, it will make the job of marketing and selling to the government efficient and effective for your company. Defining what to market and sell will increase your chances of having successful meetings with the government staff. It will also increase your chance of winning a contract and help to start the company branding process. In addition, you must perform on your first contract in an outstanding manner to increase your chances of receiving future awards. If you do not start the government sales process by defining your product, it will be very difficult to succeed in the government market sector. However, if you define your products and services and match them to the right agency, you will increase your chances of being successful in this endeavor.

CHAPTER 5

HIRING A CONSULTANT

Many companies question whether they should hire a business development or capture consultant for marketing to the federal government. This is a budget buster question for small and or medium-sized businesses. Hiring business development or capture consultants can be expensive and tricky, especially for small businesses. It is essential that you have business development or capture consultants on your team who are experts of government contracting. If you hire the right business development or capture consultant, it should help you land a government contract.

One of the first questions to ask in regards to business development and capture consultants is whether they have the right skill sets for your company. In my years of buying products and services for the government, I have observed that there are two types of business development and capture consultants. They include:

- Skill Set #1: A retired senior level official/technical expert who knows a lot of other senior federal officials and can get you into the door to meet them.
- Skill Set #2: A representative who knows what is going on in various agencies and knows the tools, techniques and the right personnel to help you win a government contract.

Both of these potential employees have pros and cons. You need to decide which one is right for you, and which one gives your company the best chances of winning a government contract.

A RETIRED SENIOR LEVEL OFFICIAL/TECHNICAL EXPERT

A retired senior level official/technical expert (skill set #1) who knows a lot of people and can get you into the doors of the federal agencies has some real advantages. This person knows what is going on at their former agency or agencies, and has knowledge and skills in that particular field. A former Chief Information Officer (CIO) of a federal agency is a good example of the first skill set. He or she will know what is going on in the government in their particular area of expertise, and will also know a lot of top-level personnel. This person can get you into the doors to meet with government and contractor personnel. He or she can also help you determine what major contracting opportunities are going on now or may be taking place over the next few years at a particular agency. The CIOs, like retired military generals, consider themselves to be part of a brotherhood. You need to hire that kind of person if you want to gain quick access to the right individual(s).

A small business CEO met with me to market his services to the agency I was working with. He was a smart guy, and knew the federal government contract business very well. He graduated from the SBA 8(a) Set-Aside Program and was winning most of his work through GSA Schedule awards. He was a good marketer, but would still hire retired senior-level officials for short durations to get access to the right people in his targeted federal agencies. By hiring the right type of sales representative on an as-needed basis, he was limiting his cost exposure while achieving his objective. This was a good business model.

There are some disadvantages to hiring the former senior level executive. First, they are very expensive. I would consider hiring them on a part-time, 1099 basis to determine what they can do for you. If you have government cost reimbursement contracts and the government is paying your indirect costs, you might want to hire them full-time. Another potential disadvantage to full-time employment is that they may talk a good game, but may be ineffective in helping you win government contracts. They also may not be well-liked among their peers or the agency you want to target. They need to have good people skills to get you into the door, and not everyone at the top of the management chain in the federal government actually has good people skills. In addition, they may not share your goal of winning government contracts. They may seek only to prove to you who they know, and provide no value to help you win government contracts.

Finally, since they were senior government staff, they may think that they can manage your business better than you. Do not fall into that trap, as they may suck you dry of your cash flow. You are the one hunting for a federal contract, and it is your company that fails without a contract. If your company fails, the former senior level official may continue to receive a government pension. You must make sure that their goals match your goals before you hire them. Due to their limitations, including cost, you need to pick them very carefully. Do not be afraid to let them go if they are not helping you to achieve your objective. You should have targets and goals for them, just like you would with anyone else in your company. Targets and goals should be included in their contract, even when they are reimbursed for their services with a retainer agreement.

You can increase your sales without these individuals, but you will have to hunt and work a little harder. Employ these individuals to help you to understand what initiatives are being implemented at your targeted agencies and to get you access to the appropriate individuals at the agencies. If they are not doing that in an efficient and effective manner, they are wasting your time and money. If these former senior level officials have unique skill sets that will help you land a contract, you should hire them. Hire them only if it is right for your company and the specific situation.

In 2010, I was at the Walter Reed Medical Center in Bethesda for a job fair recruiting disabled military veterans. Walter Reed was in the process of closing the facility, and my office wanted to hire military personnel who may have the skills sets to become acquisition professionals. I met a man at the job fair who was in his early forties and dressed professionally in a suit and tie. Initially, he did not approach me, but he did eventually. He was cautious because he knew that I was a government contracting officer. He was looking for a job as a government employee, but also owned a company that was hunting for government contracts. He had three young children and needed a job until his business was up and running. The company was functioning as a subcontractor in the federal market sector, but had difficultly becoming a prime contractor. His lack of business development knowledge and capture management skills was a big stumbling block. I thought that his chance of success was very limited due to his limited skills marketing and selling his company to federal contracting and program officials. In my discussion with him, he expressed very limited knowledge of how to market and sell to the government. His start-up company did not have adequate resources to hire a business development consultant. If he had the cash flow or could have had hired the right retired senior level official, he would have significantly increased his chances of success.

Geography can also play a major role in selecting the right consultant. A large number of federal agency buildings are located in the Washington D.C. area. If the majority of your targeted agency's contract awards are made by contracting officials in the Washington D.C. area and your company is not located close to Washington D.C., you should hire a business development or capture consultant who lives close to Washington D.C. area. They will have better access to the government offices, and will be available to attend meetings about contracting opportunities. They will also be able to develop an array of professional, face-to-face relationships with both federal and contractor personnel at your targeted agencies that may not have been otherwise accessible to your company.

BUSINESS DEVELOPMENT/CAPTURE CONSULTANTS

The other type of expert is a lower level business development/capture consultant (skill set #2). A true business development/capture consultant knows what is going on in various federal agencies. They also know the various tools, techniques, and names of personnel at all levels in an agency to help you win a government contract. They are your typical sales staff with a twist; their sales expertise is specific to government contracting. They can help you find work using the tools and techniques that are described in this book. Any business development expert/capture consultant will need to work more hours for you than the former senior level officials because they have a broader skill set. They can perform multiple tasks including interpreting the FAR, developing proposal strategies, preparing proposals, and performing business development activities.

A good business development/capture consultant knows just as much as the former senior level officials regarding the agencies you want to target. They may not be as successful in getting your company the same access, but will know who you need to talk to gain that access. They know their way around the lower organizational levels in an agency, which may be better than meeting with the senior level officials. Senior level federal officials generally meet with the large contractors, who have a known performance record and know how to operate with federal agencies. It may be difficult for small and medium sized contractors to meet with the senior level federal officials without the right business development expert.

A contractor executive stated that prior to hiring former government employees for business development work, they would bring the potential employee(s) to a Panera Bread located next the targeted agency. The agency personnel frequented the Panera Bread for morning coffee between 8:00 and 10:00 a.m. If the potential business development employee(s) knew a lot of the agency's current employees by name, and they appeared to like him/her, they would hire the retired employee. If the potential business development employee did not appear to know a lot of the employees and/or the employees did not appear to like the individual, they were not further considered for the position. This is one technique a company used to screen retired government employees for business development/capture activities.

Capture consultants in particular are like gold prospectors. They chip away at the federal agencies and eventually help you find a nugget in regards to information and contacts. Nugget after nugget will ideally lead to winning federal government contracts. These consultants will free up your precious time to allow you to adequately manage your company. They know the federal government processes, rules and regulations better than anyone in the marketplace. They are specialized to help you meet your sales objectives. Just be careful when you hire them because some of the business development and capture consultants may claim to know how to help you win government contracts, but really do not. If you do not pick the person with the right skills sets, you will be wasting your company's resources.

Business development and capture consultants use their knowledge, skills, abilities, and relationships, developed over their career, to help you win government contracts. When hiring individuals with these skill sets, establish goals and track the goals to ensure that they are being met. If you do not gain immediate benefits in terms of knowledge of your targeted agencies, you should consider hiring a different business development or capture consultant. Remember that these skill sets are hard to find in the marketplace. Be selective when hiring business development or capture consultants because a skilled one is a rare find. Many of them in the marketplace will not have the right skill sets to help you win a contract.

CONSULTANTS ARE EXPENSIVE

The business development and capture consultants are often very expensive. However, remember that if you receive a government cost-type contract, the government will pay for some or all of your indirect costs. These personnel can be included in the indirect cost pool. This type of contract will help fund business development and capture consultants. However, the costs must be reasonable to ensure reimbursement from the government. Before you hire someone, determine your needs and pick them carefully because skilled business development or capture consultants are hard to find, regardless of the cost.

BEFORE HIRING THAT CONSULTANT

Before hiring any consultant to help your company win new business, there is a non-profit professional association representing the 'front half' of the Federal Business Development Life Cycle (FBDLC). It's the Professional Capture Management Forum (www.ProCM.org), and it is a totally volunteer association. ProCM represents federal business development (BD), capture, solution architecting, and pricing strategy. These four disciplines are THE TEAM necessary to win new federal business. Their in-depth business development training and professional certification is an industry 'First' and includes 60 days of free mentoring and coaching. Through this training ProCM dismisses the myth that if a company hires a well-connected business developer, they can win a contact in 6 months. This simply is not true.

ProCM seminars primarily target small, in-between and mid-sized companies where the competition is extremely fierce. They also help large prime contractors to educate and better utilize their small business teammates become more effective in generating IDIQ revenue. Everyone, prime, small business partners, and the government win in this scenario.

Another critical aspect of their training is learning how to: identify, recruit, hire, manage, and measure successful federal business development professionals. Many small, in-between and mid-size contractors make a misstep in this area costing them hundreds of thousands of dollars and getting no return on their investment.

They have an independent certification board and are hoping to have their curriculum added to Graduate and Professional Studies Program at a Virginia university in the near future.

CHAPTER 6

FIND YOUR TARGETED AGENCY

After you have determined what you want to sell, filled out the various forms and thought about hiring a consultant, you are ready to move forward. Before you can sell to the government, you must determine which agency needs that product or service. Your mission is to gather information and determine which agency you want to target. You may have a range of reasons for targeting a specific agency, including the agency's need for your products or services, the agency's proximity to your residence, a personal passion for the services the agency provides to the public, and even your knowledge of the particular agency. Whatever the reason, you need to locate the right agency for your product or service.

There are fifteen different departments in the Executive Branch of the federal government. In all, there are over one hundred separate federal agencies in each of these departments. The departments include:

- Department of Agriculture
- Department of Commerce
- Department of Defense
- Department of Education
- Department of Energy
- Department of Health and Human Services
- Department of Homeland Security
- Department of Housing and Urban Development
- Department of Justice
- Department of Labor
- Department of State

- Department of the Interior
- Department of the Treasury
- Department of Transportation
- Department of Veterans Affairs

BASIC TARGET INFORMATION: GOVERNMENT SOURCES

If you know that an agency needs your products and services, you are off to a good start. If you do not know if an agency needs your products and services, you may be wasting your time and resources soliciting that agency. Regardless, there are easy ways to find out.

The three primary government sources of information for determining an agency's procurement needs are the Federal Business Opportunities (FedBizOpps) website at https://www.fbo.gov/, the Federal Procurement Data System (FPDS) website at https://www.FPDS.gov, and the USA Spending website at http://www.USAspending.gov.

The FedBizOpps site lists active federal government solicitations (government requests for bids and proposals), and also allows you to review archived solicitations. The website has training links to help you learn how to use the website, including tutorials explaining how to search for information. This process can be time consuming, but will be worth your effort. This website will help you determine whether an agency is soliciting your products and services, and whether they have bought them in the past. However, a lot of agency procurement actions are not listed in the FedBizOpps. I will discuss the FedBizOpps in more detail in the preceding chapters.

Another great source of information is the Federal Procurement Data System website. In an effort to make the government more transparent, federal agencies are required to put all contract award information into a database. Federal contracting officials are required to input almost all of their contract award information above the micro purchase threshold ($3,000 in 2014) into the FPDS database. This database contains award information going back to Fiscal Year 2004.

You can search this site rather than the FedBizOpps to discover award information and determine which agency is buying your products and services. This database allows you to sort the award information in many ways, including by agency, NAICS codes, state, county, small business awards, etc. If you use this website correctly, you should be able to determine whether an agency needs your products and services. However, this website does not provide a detailed breakdown of what is being procured. Therefore, you will need to perform additional tasks to acquire the detail. I will describe how to acquire this information in a subsequent chapter.

Another good website is USAspending.gov. It was launched in December 2007 by the Office of Management and Budget to include the following information: the name of the entity receiving the award; the amount of the award; information on the award including transaction type, funding agency, etc.; the location of the entity receiving the award; and a unique identifier of the entity receiving the award. Prime award information shown on the website is provided by federal agencies. USAspending.gov displays data pertaining to award amounts during a given budget period. It also includes first-tier sub-award data for subcontracts and subgrants. USAspending.gov receives its data from the information entered into the FPDS and various federal grant systems.

Federal agencies all have websites. You must check the agency's website to determine if there is information that describes how an agency buys its products and services.

You should look for a website link to their acquisition and small business offices. This should provide you with basic information that you can use to determine how they procure products and services.

BASIC TARGET INFORMATION: COMMERCIAL SOURCES

There are also ways to get information from commercial sources. In many cases, you will have to pay for this information. The most often used commercial sources of government contract information are products and services offered by Deltek and Bloomberg Government. These companies charge a fee for access to their information and services.

Deltek has many government contracting research related products. In particular, Deltek's product, GOVWIN, has been in the marketplace for a long time. GOVWIN helps to identify contracting opportunities and provides an industry analysis of federal, state, and local governments. GOVWIN's product line provides insight of federal opportunities using a centralized and detailed platform at the pre-award and post-award contracting stages. This product helps you save time and hunt in advance for the right opportunities. GOVWIN will even support you to find teaming partners. Review GOVWIN's website (http://www.deltek.com/products/govwin) to understand all of their contracting tools.

In addition to GOVWIN, there is a relatively new product in the marketplace called Bloomberg Government (BGOV). BGOV is a comprehensive web-based tool that uses data, in-depth analysis, news, directories, and integrated analytical tools to help business development staff. The BGOV website states "Through the web-based application, users can examine all federal legislative, regulatory and contracting activities, in an easily searchable format. This provides clients with all the information they need to perform their work within one easy to navigate tool, allowing them to move quickly and efficiently with a clear understanding of the ever-evolving, complex government landscape. BGOV eliminates the need for multiple information services and the associated costs, saves time and delivers the insights clients need to make better, faster decisions." You can find information on their website at http://about.bgov.com/.

Additional free commercial sources include internet sites, magazine articles, newspaper articles, company public announcements, the local Chamber of Commerce, and associations of similar business entities. Your state small business office may also have resources available to help find state government opportunities.

TARGET BASED ON PROXIMITY TO YOUR RESIDENCE

We all want a great quality of life. Commuting to and from a federal facility by car or air requires time that could be spent on your business or with your family. Before you begin hunting for government work, target the agencies that are close to your home. You will be better able to win and manage a government contract if you are located close to the specific government facility. You will also be readily available to meet with government officials before and after the contract award if you are located near the targeted agency.

One important technique that I will recommend in a later chapter is to obtain a badge that allows you unrestricted access to a federal facility. Federal agencies have various requirements for obtaining a badge. If you have access to the federal buildings at your targeted agency on a regular day-to-day and week-to-week basis, you may be eligible to receive an access badge. However, you cannot do this if you do not live in close proximity to the federal buildings. If you do receive a government building access badge, it may improve your opportunities to gather information and build relationships with government officials, which may lead to additional contract awards. It is a distinct advantage being located in close proximity to your targeted agency.

If you are not located close to the agency that you are targeting, you may want to find office space and hire personnel in the area to gain access to the agency. If you land a big contract, it will be to your advantage to find personnel located in the area. They can help you find a reasonably priced location and hire personnel in the local area.

A capture consultant recently told me that the Chief Operating Officer of his company told his capture staff that if they wanted to target a particular agency that is located outside of the Washington D.C. Beltway, they had to be physically located there. He knew that being located in close proximity created an advantage in the marketplace by allowing contractors to gather information, gain knowledge, and build relationship in the most efficient and effective manner. Not being located in close proximity makes it harder for any federal contractor to be successful.

TARGET BASED ON PASSION FOR A PARTICULAR AGENCY MISSION

If you have a passion for the mission of a particular agency, or a passion for a product or service that a particular agency buys, that may be the agency you should target. We all know that sales staff do a better job selling a product or service if they have passion for it. The same holds true for targeting an agency. If you have a passion for the mission of a particular agency, you will have a greater chance of winning a contract award. Stick with what you know and work according to your passion.

LIMIT THE AGENCIES YOU TARGET

I have met a lot of sales and business development staff who sell to the government. Many small and medium-sized businesses, which have millions of dollars in government sales, target only two or three agencies. That is why they are successful. Generally, only the larger companies are very successful targeting multiple departments and agencies. Many small and medium-sized companies only target a few agencies because that is how they can effectively and efficiently use their limited labor resources to hunt for work.

Federal agencies are decentralized. Each federal department has many agencies, and each agency has many facilities and offices spread out in multiple locations. Each of these locations may have its own procurement office. It is your job to find the locations of these procurement offices and learn how to get access to them. This will require some research on your part. Check the Internet, the yellow pages, your local Chamber of Commerce, and your business contacts to gather information regarding local government agencies.

TARGET BASED ON KNOWLEDGE OF AN AGENCY

If you have previous knowledge about a federal agency, then that may be the agency to target. Previous knowledge could come from prior employment, working for a contractor or through your own education or awareness about an agency. Knowledge regarding how federal agencies function and manage their contracts is priceless information and normally takes years to acquire. If you already have this knowledge and you have a product or service that the agency needs, target that agency. Knowledge about an agency can also make the latest agency information easier to process and understand. Target an agency you know first, and use that knowledge in the future to help you identify how other agencies function.

Even though you have found your targeted agency, the process of gaining knowledge, gathering information, and building relationships remains. It is a never ending process. However, each time you gain knowledge and information about one agency, it will become easier to gain knowledge and information at the next agency.

CHAPTER 7

OBTAIN DETAILED KNOWLEDGE ABOUT YOUR TARGETED AGENCY

Once you have decided to target an agency to sell your products or services, you need to learn as much about that agency as possible. Government contracting begins and ends with gathering information. Knowledge and information about your targeted agency is power and will be a major key to your initial and continued success in government contracting. Gathering information and research always starts with being organized. You must gather the information regarding your targeted agency, organize it in database files and share it with your team. Leverage what other members on your team know, who they know and how you can use those contacts. Once you have started gathering and organizing data, you will acquire a clear idea of how the targeted agency functions and is organizationally structured. This step should be sufficiently completed before you submit a proposal in response to a solicitation at your targeted agency. When you have gained significant knowledge of your targeted agency, you will be able to move to the next steps in your government contracting journey.

WHAT INFORMATION DO YOU NEED TO KNOW?

Although you need as much information as possible about your targeted agency, the information you need to know will always depend on the products and services that you are marketing to the government. Some of the basic information you need to know could be:

- What federal programs are initiated by an agency?

- What new initiatives are taking place at the agency?
- Where are the targeted agency's contracting and program offices physically located?
- When do the agency's current contracts for your products and services expire?
- What contractors are currently supplying the agency with your products and services?
- What contracting vehicles does the agency use to procure your products and services?
- How does the agency write statements of work or product specifications?
- What were the technical evaluation criteria in previous solicitations?
- What NAICS codes is the agency using for your products and services?
- Is it easy to access staff at the agency?
- What outreach activities are used to communicate with contractors?
- What contract types/pricing methodologies are used?
- Will your current accounting system support the contracting methods used by the agency?

AGENCY WEBSITES

Federal agencies are very complex organizations. Federal agencies update their websites with their mission, programs and other aspects of how they function to educate the public. There is a lot of valuable information on an agency's website, but these sites can also be overwhelming. Start by finding answers to the questions listed above and become familiar with your targeted agency's website. Familiarity of an agency website will result in easier navigation and understanding of an agency's programs and missions.

Each agency's website will present a lot of information including bid lists for micro-purchases, new initiatives, descriptions of the programs, outreach and education activities, events and conferences, training initiatives, and regulations. You can spend weeks searching an agency's website to gather information. Although this is time consuming, the information may not be found in another place.

Do not try to contact the agency's staff immediately, even if you have the basic information. The contracting office personnel that you need to meet at an agency are generally overwhelmed with work and understaffed. There are not enough hours in the day for them to know every initiative that is taking place in an agency. To be successful, you need to help them, and make their job easier rather than harder. I will explain how to do this in Chapter 12. Continue searching the agency's website and research the initiatives that are currently proceeding at an agency.

You should be able to find information about major initiatives on an agency's website. This will help you begin to connect the dots in order to draw up a marketing plan. Go to the website and try to ascertain whether any of the initiatives involve work that is in your company's area of expertise. For example, if there is information on an army base's website concerning a base realignment, you know that there will be a lot of new construction initiatives. If you find information regarding the implementation of new Medicare laws, rules, and regulations, there may be a lot of computer programming activities required to implement them. These clues give you a good place to start.

The HHS agencies provide detailed information on the internet regarding their current fiscal year programs and budgets. The HHS titles the reports "Justification for

Estimates for the Appropriations Committees." The reports contain over two hundred pages of information for each HHS agency. The reports explain the agency's programs and budgets in an easy to understand, yet detailed manner. A capture consultant informed me that he recommends his clients use this document for gaining information about their target agencies. If you are unfamiliar with all of your targeted agency's programs or budgets, these HHS documents will help you to quickly learn a lot of valuable information about your targeted agency. I recommend you look for similar publicly available documents at your targeted agency to gain valuable information.

There are also government websites available that are not specific to a particular agency that may help you find information about your targeted agency. For example, www.contractdirectory.gov is one such database. It is a database used to identify existing contracts and other contract instruments that can be used by multiple federal agencies. You can use this site to determine what multiple award contracts are available in the marketplace.

The agency websites probably will not have procurement announcements, but may have a bulletin board page for posting small procurements. Procurements under $30,000 do not have to be posted on the FedBizOpps, but should appear on the agency's website. The website will give you an idea of the agency's processes used to procure small purchases. It presents an opportunity if you are hunting for small procurements. Large procurements are often published on the FedBizOpps. Agency websites are only good if they are reasonably well organized and provide you with information to gain knowledge about the agency.

OFFICE OF MANAGEMENT AND BUDGET EXHIBIT 300

One significant way to gain knowledge regarding a federal agency's future contracts is to gather information early in the federal budget process. One way to gain knowledge about federal agency information technology (IT) investments early in the budget process is reviewing the Office of Management and Budget (OMB) Exhibit 300 submissions for your targeted agency. The OMB Exhibit 300s are the backbone of planning, budgeting, acquisition, and management of major IT capital investments at each federal agency. Agencies must submit a OMB Exhibit 300 for each major capital IT project to demonstrate they are utilizing sound project management techniques, developing strong business cases for the IT investment, and defining the proposed cost, schedule, and performance goals.

The OMB Exhibit 300s are submitted by an agency to their department and to the Office of Management and Budget early in the budget formulation process. It is submitted in the subsequent fiscal year for the Congressional approval process and again in the next fiscal year for an agency's budget execution process. As a result, OMB Exhibit 300s tracks IT investments through the budget formulation and approval process, and all the way through the contract awards and an IT projects life cycle. The budget formulation process begins two years prior to Congress and the President approving the current fiscal year budget. In addition to the OMB Exhibit 300, an Exhibit 53 is used to document budget estimates for major IT systems of each agency. The website for the OMB Exhibit 300s is https://itdashboard.gov/. The website contains actual costs expended in the prior fiscal year, estimates for the current fiscal year and the budget estimate for the next fiscal year. Federal agencies also have similar information on their websites.

The information on an agency's website may contain the latest or outdated information. Ideally, the OMB Exhibit 300s and Exhibit 53s that are in the budget formulation phase of the life of an IT project will provide valuable information regarding an agency's future contract priorities. As an IT investment moves through Congressional approval, the OMB Exhibit 300s and Exhibit 53s become more accurate to reflect the budget amounts approved for major IT projects. As the IT investment moves through the project execution, the OMB Exhibit 300s and Exhibit 53s reflect budget commitments in an agency in a given fiscal year. You should review the OMB Exhibit 300s and Exhibit 53s to learn as much as possible about your targeted agency's IT investments.

FEDBIZOPPS NOTICES

You can find some of an agency's published solicitation announcements on the FedBizOpps website. The website contains electronic copies of the agency's solicitations. Search in the FedBizOpps for active solicitations, archived solicitations, Sources Sought Notices, and Award Notices to assess what an agency buys. Review active FedBizOpps solicitations the agency currently has posted to determine if they regularly use FedBizOpps to procure your products and services. Review the Source Sought Notices to determine whether the agency is currently searching for products and services that you can deliver. Additionally, review the agency's Award Notices to determine if contract awards have been made for your specific products and services.

Generally, Sources Sought Notices are posted by government contracting offices in conjunction with the agency's Small Business Specialist to help determine whether particular acquisitions should be set-aside for small businesses. If interested contractors are found to be qualified in any particular small business category, the agency will consider setting that acquisition aside for small businesses. If interested contractors are found not to be qualified, the agency will make that acquisition a Full and Open Competition procurement. These notices will also help you determine which agency is buying your products and services and whether they set the procurements aside for small businesses. If an agency finds a small business that can perform the work under certain dollar thresholds, they will not post the solicitation in the FedBizOpps.

It is important to review both the request for proposal announcements and Sources Sought Notices to learn as much as possible about your targeted agency. Generally, if the agency does not locate a small business capable of performing the work for a particular solicitation, including small business set-asides, it will post the solicitation for both large and small businesses on the FedBizOpps. Both large and small businesses will then have a chance to submit proposals.

It is vital to know how an agency buys its products and services because not all requests for proposals are posted on the FedBizOpps. An agency might be buying products and services similar to yours, but do not have to post the request for proposal on the FedBizOpps. An agency is not required to post a solicitation in the FedBizOpps if they have Indefinite Delivery Indefinite Quantity (IDIQ) contracts or Blank Purchase Agreements in place, uses another agency's IDIQ contracts, buys off of the GSA Schedule (and therefore is not required to post the requirements), or uses the authority of the Small Business Act. If this is the case, you will need to use information technology tools other than the FedBizOpps to determine if an agency has solicitation and contracts for your products or services. Regarding an IDIQ contract, the initial/base contract solicitation and award notification were probably posted on the FedBizOpps, but subsequent task order solicitations are not usually posted.

Once you have used the FedBizOpps to determine if the agency has procured your products and services in the past, move to the next step. Print out the agency's previous solicitations for similar products and services and use them to outline the agency's acquisition strategies. Key points that you should review in the solicitations include the contract type, NAICS codes, pricing structure, evaluation criteria, page limitations of proposal submissions, acquisition lead times (how long did it take to award the contract after the solicitation was released), and contract terms and conditions. Reviewing past solicitations may help you to determine if you are eligible to submit a proposal for a future solicitation.

You can also review award information in the FedBizOpps to determine the contract award amounts for the products and services in the solicitations noted above. However, remember that a lot of agency contract and task order awards are not posted in the FedBizOpps. If you can find the solicitations and awards in the FedBizOpps database, you will be in a better position to propose on solicitations at your targeted agency. The FedBizOpps Award Notices include what an agency has bought at the initial award, but will not give you a guarantee that the agency is going to buy it again. The FedBizOpps does help you begin to connect more of the dots. Organize your findings by saving and/or printing the targeted agency's solicitations from the FedBizOpps to learn as much as possible.

The FedBizOpps also has postings for federal subcontracting opportunities. In addition, the website lists sales of Surplus Property and sales of Foreign Business

Opportunities; this is another way to learn who the agency uses as prime contractors. It contains a Vendor Guide and demonstration videos to help you learn how to use and maneuver through the website.

A review of the FedBizOpps is just the beginning of your endeavor to find out about your targeted agency. It is a good starter for gathering information, but it will not provide you all of the information you will need. There are other tools available to increase your knowledge and gather information.

THE FEDERAL PROCUREMENT DATA SYSTEM

The Federal Procurement Data System (FPDS) is a repository of federal government contract award information. Almost all federal government contract award information is entered into the FPDS. Contracting officials at the agencies are required to enter the contract award information into the FPDS. The FPDS includes almost all award actions greater than $3,000 including contract modifications. For example, if a contract was initially awarded for $10,000,000 and twenty-five contract modifications were issued during the five year period of performance, you will see the contract award information plus the information for each of the twenty-five contract modifications. FPDS contains more post-award information than the FedBizOpps because federal officials do not post contract modification information on the FedBizOpps website, only the initial award information. However, you can obtain copies of the full solicitations using the FedBizOpps website. You cannot duplicate copies of the solicitations or contract documents in FPDS.

The FPDS contains a summary snapshot of key contract award information that is valuable to your company. The award information is entered into the FPDS by the government contracting officer or contract specialist assigned to the contract. There are 205 potential fields of information in the FPDS. Grant and cooperative agreement information is not placed in the FPDS.

You must create an account and register into the FPDS. After a few quick steps to register, you can determine if an agency is procuring similar products and services to those you are selling.

As is noted in the FPDS User's Manual, some of the key information that the agency officials electronically input into the FPDS system includes:

- Contract Number
- Current Completion Date
- Ultimate Completion Date
- Contracting Agency Code
- Type of Contract
- Government Furnished Property
- Place of Manufacture
- Extent Competed
- Number of Offers Received
- Type of Set-Aside
- FedBizOpps Notice
- Reason for Modification
- Vendor Name
- Email Address of Contractor and Government Personnel

This information is just a slice of the data contained in the FPDS. The types of appropriated fund awards that are reportable to the FPDS include:

- Replenishable stock and revolving funds
- Funds being transferred from one executive agency to another, where the servicing agency contracts for the supplies or services

- Funding obligated pursuant to the provisions of PL 85-804
- Interagency Transfers of funding
- Funds for supplies and equipment
- Funds for construction, alteration or maintenance of real property
- Funds for services, including research and development and utilities
- Funds for AbilityOne (formerly JWOD Nonprofit Agency or Sheltered Workshop awards)
- Funds for telecommunications from regulated carriers
- Funds for Federal Prison Industries, i.e. UNICOR awards (orders from GSA stock for UNICOR products are not reportable)
- Funds held in trust accounts for foreign governments or procurements for foreign governments regardless of the nature of the funds

The following information is not reported in FPDS:

- Financial assistance actions, e.g. grants, cooperative agreements
- Impress fund transactions, SF 44 purchases, training authorizations, and micro-purchases obtained through the use of the government purchase card
- Interagency agreements with other federal agencies.
- Government Bills of Lading and Government Transportation Requests
- Actions using predominantly non-appropriated funds, except pursuant to funds held in trust accounts mentioned
- FEDSTRIP and MILSTRIP requisitions
- Actions involving transfer of supplies within and among agencies and sub-agencies
- Orders from GSA Stock and GSA Consolidated Purchase Program.

73

- Petroleum or petroleum products ordered against a Defense Logistics Agency Indefinite Delivery Contract

The FPDS does not collect:

- Subcontractor data
- Accounting data
- Contract line item data including information about individual Contract Line Items Numbers in a contract award (CLINs data)
- Administrative details
- Details of the contractor's employee or staffing levels
- Management plans
- Statements of work or objectives
- Terms and conditions of a contract
- Deliverables
- Entitlement expenditures
- Contractor proposals from the awardee or any other interested party
- Information about any parties excluded from the procurement

If you are not using the FPDS, your competition is a step ahead of you. Your sales staff and/or business development staff must use the FPDS. Your competition is using it. In late 2011 and early 2012, I told the CEO of a small business contractor and later a business development consultant the virtues of the FPDS. They had both been doing government contracting for years, yet were totally unfamiliar with it. Within a month, I received an email from the CEO's employee who was instructed to use the FPDS. This employee found the FPDS to be very informative and it significantly increased the knowledge base for the company.

The business development employee asked how many task orders were awarded on a particular contract. I explained that I could not provide him with this information, but he could find it on the FPDS's website. I also informed him that the FPDS's website has a tutorial to help him learn how to gather information on the FPDS. Within one day, he emailed me stating that the FPDS is a useful tool which allowed him to compile the information that he needed.

In another example of the value of FPDS, in January 2013, I received a telephone call from an 8(a) contractor who began his government contracting business in 2012. In early 2012, I briefed him about the benefits of the FPDS and explained how to hunt for government contracts using it. Specifically, I told him to find the 8(a) contract awards in the FPDS that were awarded over the previous five years at his targeted agency. I requested he review the information and determine which contracts were ending in the near future. I then told him to use the information in the FPDS to contact the contracting officer and/or the COR. He contacted the COR assigned to the expiring 8(a) contract and provided his company's capabilities. He later told me that he received a $2.5 million contract using this technique.

I was at a National Contract Management Association Networking event in early 2015 and I was having a discussion with the CEO of a company and their business development consultant. The company employed 25 personnel. The business development consultant had been performing business development activities for many years. They had four years remaining in the 8(a) program and had been in the 8(a) program for five years. They did not know what the FPDS was and how it could be used to help the company market and sell to the government. They were missing a key tool needed to gain information about their targeted agency.

The data contained in FPDS is a great informational tool. You should use the FPDS website to find out as much information as possible about your targeted agency. The FPDS has some significant advantages compared to FedBizOpps. By using the FPDS, you will save time and money gathering information.

FREEDOM OF INFORMATION ACT REQUESTS

Once you have obtained general contract award information in the FPDS, your next step is to secure actually copies of contract awards including contract modifications. The Freedom of Information Act (FOIA) is a federal law that allows you to receive the actual copies of contract award information at any federal government agency.

FOIA is a federal law that gives any person, including U.S. citizens, foreign nationals, organizations, associations and universities, the right to obtain information from a federal government agency. In accordance with the http://www.foia.gov website, you can obtain agency records such as contract award information (including contract modifications), print documents, photographs, videos, maps, emails, and electronic records that were created or obtained by a federal agency and are, at the time you file a request, in that agency's possession and control. The agency is required to respond to your FOIA in twenty days or notify you if they cannot respond in that time due to certain circumstances. Under President Obama, federal agencies have added FOIA staff to eliminate the backlog of FOIA requests. As a result, federal agencies are now doing their best to respond to FOIA requests in twenty days. You can use the information in the FPDS to provide the information you need to submit a FOIA request to an agency.

Give yourself as much lead time as possible in regards to requesting contract award documents because some federal agencies are months behind in processing their FOIA requests. Go to the agency's website to find FOIA submission information. When you submit the request(s) to an agency, you will be assigned an employee who is responsible for processing your request(s).

You should always request copies of contract awards and contract modifications using the specific contract number that you found in the FPDS. Contract modifications will give you valuable information. For instance, if an agency awards a five year contract and you submit a FOIA request in the third year of the contract, you will gain insight into additional work that was added to the contract over the period of performance. The FOIA helps to level the playing field and reduces the competitive advantage that incumbent contractors have at your targeted agency by providing copies of the actual contract documents including contract modifications.

There are some reasons why the FOIA-requested information, otherwise known as "exceptions," cannot be released to a requestor. In general, you will not receive copies of your competitor's proposals if they won a previously awarded contract. You may not receive copies of contractors' technical or business proposals (confidential business information) if the proposals were not referenced or incorporated in the government contract. Government contract officials should no longer be referencing a contractor's technical proposal in a contract. If they do, you can get access to your competitor's proposal with the proprietary information blacked-out. Search the internet for the "FOIA Exceptions" and you will easily find the information that the government officials will not release through the FOIA.

AGENCY ORGANIZATIONAL STRUCTURE

Federal government agencies for the most part are very complex organizations. Your basic knowledge of an agency must include a sound foundation of how your targeted agency is organizationally structured and where your products and services fit into the organizational structure. Knowing the structure helps you to effectively gather information and potentially build relationships with the personnel in an agency. The primary tool for gaining this knowledge is a detailed organizational chart. A detailed organizational chart will probably list the names of the federal managers responsible for every area in an agency. It is very important that you gain access to an organizational chart to obtain information about your targeted agency.

Organizational chart information can be gathered from many sources. Each agency's website may have a chart of its own, and these charts may also be available at various agency conferences. You can ask for an organizational chart through a FOIA request. You can also try to find them free of charge, from internet sources such as http://wikiorgcharts.com/. This is a free open-source website that collects public and private company's organizational charts. If you have organizational charts, you can post them on the website for others to have access to as well. Many private companies, like GovWin and Carroll Publishing, also sell organizational charts. If you want to save time, I suggest that you buy the charts from vendors in the marketplace.

Most agencies do not release their organizational chart information because they do not want their employees being contacted by hundreds of contractors. Federal agencies may also change the organizational structure and personnel at the senior level positions relatively often, making the charts outdated. However, even a recently outdated organizational chart will provide you with valuable information.

NAME AND PHONE NUMBERS OF FEDERAL OFFICIALS

You should also work to find the names, telephone numbers and email addresses of the federal personnel at your targeted agency. Managerial staff names should be listed on the organizational charts, though the charts usually will not have information of non-managerial personnel. You can find the individual's names from other sources, including the FPDS or from actual contract documents. Managerial and staff personnel telephone numbers may sometimes be accessed on the internet, though some agencies guard this information more closely than others. For example, Department of Health and Human Services (HHS) lists employee telephone numbers at http://directory.psc.gov/employee.htm. This website includes telephone and email addresses of personnel for a number of agencies in the HHS, including the National Institutes of Health, the Food and Drug Administration, and the Centers for Medicare and Medicaid. Your targeted agency may do the same.

If you cannot find the email address of a federal official, but know their name, you can often determine their email address. Federal agencies use similar patterns of email addresses and are based on employee names. Find the name of at least two random personnel at your targeted agency on the FedBizOpps's website, FPDS's website, or other internet sources and review their email addresses. Review their email addresses to determine the email address pattern used at the targeted agency. Once you understand the email address pattern at your targeted agency, all you need to know is the name of a person at the targeted agency to email them. Understanding an agency's email pattern will help you to contact personnel at your targeted agency.

This chapter provided you with the tools and techniques required to gather basic information about your targeted agency. It is important that the information you gather be properly organized and stored in a database. Gaining knowledge and gathering information is an ongoing process in government contracting. The information that you gather may overwhelm you if it is not properly organized and easily accessible to the appropriate personnel in your organization.

CHAPTER 8

DEVELOP A DETAILED SALES PLAN

It takes a lot of knowledge, hard work and team effort to win a government contract. Since government contracting requires a team effort, contractor business development staffs often have very little control in regards to meeting their sales dollar goals as set by management. The sales staff cannot control federal budget cuts, changing legislation, or how and when the government personnel decide to initiate and execute a contract. As a result, the sales plan for your targeted agency must include many performance measures rather than just a sales dollar goal to accurately assess the sales staff's performance.

I have met and brainstormed with hundreds of government sales staff and almost all of them have sales dollar goals. What amazes me about the sales dollar goals is that these goals are educated guesses based on the previous year's sales. They do not usually reflect the present day reality of their targeted agency. In federal government contracting, I have witnessed sales staff exceed their sales goal by a few hundred percentage points in one year, but it comes with consequences. They blow out the sales goals one year, the earning accelerators kick-in and they make a lot of money. The next year, their sales goals increase significantly. However, as a result of factors beyond their control, their actual dollar sales drop drastically at their targeted agency. Their sales goals were unrealistic and did not reflect and account for their hard work and job performance during their fiscal year.

81

The government sales process is not very organized in some companies, regardless of the company's size. I have witnessed very few organizations that appropriately develop sales measurement tools beyond the bottom line numbers. One year, I observed a company that had over $100 million in contract awards and had only one salesperson with a sales goal of $5 million per year. Does that make sense? In this particular case, the CEO was eventually removed from his position. Sales dollar goals often create untenable situations for the sales staff and company. Bottom line dollar sales goals are not effective tools for measuring performance of salespersons. Federal government contracting can often be unpredictable, and leads to salespersons becoming burnt-out, hopping from job to job, and riding a roller coaster of job dissatisfaction.

Bottom line dollar sales goals cannot help you determine whether the salespersons are working effectively. Here is an example. Your company wins a big contract with an agency for a five-year period. After the award, your company hires a salesperson to manage the contract and increase the contract value. A new law is passed by Congress and as a result the agency in question has to substantially increase the size and scope of the contract. Your salesperson earns a substantial commission for increasing the value of the contract. Did the salesperson help to increase the sales of the company? Your answer is as good as mine, but in this example, I think that the salesperson was simply in the right place at the right time and provided little value in helping to secure the increase in the dollar value of the contract. Therefore, the bottom line dollar sales goal did not provide support in determining if the salesperson was effective in the performance period.

A close friend of mine worked as a salesperson for a large IT company in the 1980s when personal computers were just coming to the marketplace in large quantities. A large IT contractor won a contract to supply a federal agency with all of its personal computers. The agency needed thousands of computers and it was a big multi-million dollar contract. The large IT contractor's contract was an Indefinite Delivery Indefinite Quantity contract, and they were the only supplier of the personal computers for this agency. The salesperson was hired just after the contract was awarded. It was his responsibility to keep the government agency's officials happy and make sure that they continued ordering more personal computers. His sales commissions in the 1980s from this contract were a very, very significant amount of money. The federal agency continued to buy personal computers on this contract for six years. Personally, I was happy for the salesperson. He was a very effective salesperson, but professionally, I thought that the salesperson was in the right place at the right time and had little impact on what the federal agency procured.

I have also seen the opposite scenario occur. In this situation, the salespersons were seasoned veterans with excellent skill sets in federal business development and capture management. Even though they were skilled professionals, their sales dollar goals were guesses rather than realistic sales estimates of their targeted agency. One year, their targeted agency had a large budget as a result of many new legislative initiatives. The next year, the agency's budget was significantly reduced, yet the sales dollar goals remained the same. As a result of situations similar to these, in which sales dollar goals are not met, salesperson's work attitudes become negative and personal lives also become stressed. Ultimately, valued and knowledgeable salespersons are forced to leave or voluntarily find new employment.

THE NEED FOR A DETAILED SALES PLAN

There are only so many techniques a salesperson can use to win a government contract. They do not usually write the technical proposal; they are not responsible for their company's performance; and they do not have the final say in the pricing methodology. In addition, they do not have control over an agency's budget or how an agency uses its budget. Therefore, the sales staffs are responsible for meeting the sales dollar goals, but they have little control over many other factors. Smart companies solve this problem by developing detailed sales plans to effectively and efficiently measure the performance of their sales staff. I not going to tell you how to structure the plan, but I will recommend measures that should be included in the plan.

IDENTIFYING OPPORTUNITIES

The first measure includes the sales staff's ability to identify opportunities from readily available sources. As noted in previous chapters, sales staff must do their basic homework including reviewing agencies websites, the FPDS, the FedBizOpps notices, printed articles, GovWin tools or Bloomberg Government tools, and ascertain whether there are opportunities for your company. The opportunities found from these sources as well as additional sources should be submitted by the sales staff to management in the form of a deliverable on a weekly, monthly or quarterly basis. This process will help to evaluate the sales staff's ability to identify opportunities.

MEETING WITH THE SMALL BUSINESS SPECIALIST

Small business's sales staff must meet with agencies Small Business Specialists to identify future procurement

84

opportunities. The sales staff must document the name of the Small Business Specialist they met with and record the results of the meeting. The sales staff may have additional meetings with agency staff as a result of meeting the Small Business Specialist. The opportunities resulting from the meeting with the small business specialist and other agency personnel should also be submitted as a deliverable by the sales staff to management. This deliverable will assist in measuring the sales staff's ability to gather information and build relationships.

EMAIL RESULTS

Assessing email traffic is another performance measure for sales staff. They can be evaluated based on how many emails were sent out and how many responses were received from government personnel and other potential leads. If the sales staff received responses in return, it is a good indication that they are developing relationships with the targeted agency's staff. Remember, this business is all about gathering information and developing relationships. If your sales staff are not sending emails and/or receiving responses, it could be an indication that they are not effectively performing their job. The results should be submitted on a monthly or quarterly basis.

MEETINGS WITH GOVERNMENT STAFF

Documenting how many meetings your sales staff had with government officials regarding current and future acquisitions is another effective performance measure. Face-to-face meeting are more effective to build relationships and give your company name recognition. If your sales staffs are getting face-to-face time with a government customer, they are performing a job well done.

If they are conducting telephone calls with government staff concerning current or future acquisitions, it is also a job well done. If they know the government staff on a personal level and have developed a relationship, a telephone meeting is just as good as a face-to-face meeting. However, if they did not establish a professional relationship with the government personnel and only communicated once, they may not be building relationships or gathering sufficient information. This information should be tracked on a monthly or quarterly basis.

During both face-to-face and telephone meetings, sales staff should document specific aspects of their performance. Did they talk to a decision maker at the agency? Was the agency official knowledgeable regarding future acquisitions? Did the initial meeting lead to other contacts and additional meetings? If the salespersons are meeting with agency personnel, management must ascertain if they collected the appropriate information. If they are meeting with agency officials and are not asking the appropriate questions, they are not performing effectively. Measure the information they gathered from each face-to-face or telephone meeting to measure their effectiveness.

SALES STAFF CAN CREATE PERFORMANCE MEASURES

The sales staff can identify new techniques to measure their performance. They could recommend performance measures or goals based on experience at prior companies. Do not be afraid to use proven and tested techniques. On the other hand, do not be afraid to try new techniques. Your sales staffs are on the front line and they can best tell you which measures and goals can be used to effectively measure their performance. Apply some of their ideas as well as your own. Over time, the techniques that are used to measure your sales staff performance will become quite effective. The sales staff should deliver the results of their performance on a weekly, monthly or quarterly basis as appropriate using the new measures.

ASSESSING THE COMPETITION

Sales staff should know which contractors are competing for contracts at your targeted agencies. For active contracts, sales staff must know if competing incumbent contractors will continue to be eligible to perform work on contracts once they expire. They should also gather information to determine if an incumbent contractor is performing successfully. If the incumbent contractor is still able to propose on the follow-on procurement, sales staff must be able to determine the probability of winning the future solicitation. If the incumbent contractor cannot propose on the work, (including having graduated from the set-aside program or conflict of interest issues), sales staff need to know who are the other competing contractors. It may or may not be your opportunity to win a contract. Sales staff should be able to gather this information.

SUBCONTRACTING OPPORTUNITIES

You should evaluate how many subcontracting opportunities sales staff identified in a given period. This includes:

- Opportunities for your company to subcontract with a prime contractor
- Opportunities for your company to find qualified and responsible subcontractors

Sales staff must develop subcontracting opportunities for your company. These opportunities include being a subcontractor or locating subcontractors. If sales staff are

87

wheeling and dealing, it is a good indicator that they are effective representatives for your company. When the sales staff are wheeling and dealing, they are effectively gathering information and developing relationships. If sales staff develop opportunities that you do not want to be engaged in, that is okay. It is important to keep the sales staff motivated and encourage their subcontracting ideas, even if they do not materialize. The sales staff should submit the results of the potential subcontracting opportunities on a quarterly basis.

LEVERAGING RELATIONSHIPS

The sales staff's ability to leverage relationships with prime contractor personnel, subcontractor personnel and other personnel is a good indicator that they have the appropriate skill sets to help you win a government contract. Developing relationships is necessary to effectively gather information. If your sales staff is helping other sales staff outside of your company's niche, it will even pay dividends to your company in the long term. The more sales staff they know, the easier it will be to gather information to help your company win a government contract. Leveraging relationships is another performance measure of the sales staff.

ATTENDING APPROPRIATE CONFERENCES

Identify how many get-to-know conferences sales staff attended at a targeted agency, and/or how many other meetings and conferences they took part in. It is your sales staff's job to attend these meetings to build relationships and gather information. If appropriate meetings and conferences are being attended by the sales staff, measure the information gathered at them. The information should be documented so that you know that the sales staff are using the meeting and conference opportunities effectively. In addition, the information gained at the meetings and conferences can be provided to other sales staff and company officials. You must require the sales staff submit a report after attending each conference.

WIN RATIO

Identify your sales staff's success in targeting the right opportunities. If they are recommending that your company propose on government contracts that you often lose, they are not effective in determining which solicitations have the strongest possibilities for success. On the other hand, if they have gathered the appropriate information, they will be able to evaluate the chance of success on various solicitations in the federal marketplace. If you are subcontracting with another contractor, the sales staff should also know which subcontractors have a better chance of success. The sales staff's success rate can be compared to other sales staff and industry success ratios.

The win/loss ratio is used by many contractors as an indicator of successful performance. It should be measured in comparison to industry standards. Your success in the IT field may differ from the construction field. It may also vary depending on your location. If you are located in the Washington D.C. marketplace, the competition is fierce, and you have to propose on solicitations selectively. You must know the success rate for your industry, as this is a key measure for your sales staff. Your success ratio in winning government contracts will help you to determine the performance of your sales staff.

THE VALUE OF REALISTIC MEASURES

Regardless if the salesperson significantly exceeded the goals, did not meet the goals or just met the goals, a comprehensive sales and marketing plan needs to be developed for the next fiscal year. The goals may need to change if they are determined to be unattainable at any time during the year. Beside the measures suggested above, you should include other measures that are important to your company's success. Sales staff are generally good talkers and it is their job to persuade others to buy their products and services. They will do a good job trying to persuade you to see the goals and measures their way. Therefore, if you want to keep your sales staff motivated, you should seek their input and develop a competent sales plan with realistic measures.

I had a meeting with a salesperson who had targeted my agency working for two companies over the past dozen years. In a stretch of time, I had not seen him for quite a few years, but he would call me from time to time to see how I was doing and keep our relationship active. He did this even when he was not selling to my agency. He was a great salesperson, and knew how to gather information, build relationships and sell to the government. He started his own company because he had an unpleasant experience working for a small business government contractor.

This salesperson helped to increase the sales for this company and landed it a nice sized government contract, but he received only a meager commission. A small commission was not what had been verbally agreed upon with the CEO of the company. As a result, he left the company immediately and started his own company. After discussing this issue in greater depth, I realized the CEO did not recognize his talent, and did not understand his ability to build relationships, gather information, work with the customers, and market the company. In addition, there were no defined performance measures to help the CEO determine whether he was successfully performing his job. As a result, the CEO did not adequately reimburse him. He left the company and the CEO lost a valuable employee with great government business development and capture sales skills and the CEO did not even appear to know it.

USING A SALES PLAN WITH REALISTIC MEASURES

You must have realistic measures in place at your company in federal contracting to retain your sales staff. Federal government contracting can often be unpredictable. It often leads to sales staff becoming burnt out, hopping from job to job, and riding a roller coaster of dissatisfaction. It is very difficult to find good sales staff that fully understands the federal marketplace. If you place realistic measures in their sales plan, it will help you to retain your well trained sales staff in a tough marketplace.

In government contracting, the most important aspect of the sales staff's job is to gather information and build relationships. You can adequately assess their performance based on the information they have gathered and contacts they have developed over one year. Sales goals should be a piece of the sales plan, but not the only piece of the plan. A sales plan with realistic measures and documented results should also help the company to develop new sales and marketing strategies. If a lot of detailed information is gathered and relationships are developed, the company can make better decisions when considering proposing on future solicitations. It is an ongoing duty to determine if sales staff are appropriately building relationships and gathering information at the targeted agencies. This will always remain the key to your company's success.

CHAPTER 9

SMALL BUSINESS SUPPORT STAFF

A small business is defined in the Federal Acquisition Regulations, Subpart 19.3. According to the SBA website, if your organization operates for a profit, is not dominant in its field and qualifies under the size standards established by the SBA in terms of the number of employees or annual sales, then it is considered a small business. This is important for a number of reasons.

If you qualify as a small business, there are federal staff members in each department or agency available to help you. Their job is to locate and help small businesses win government contracts. Their tasks include aiding, counseling, assisting and protecting small business concerns, and they are also responsible for maximizing the opportunities for small businesses as much as possible. The personnel are called Small Business Specialists (SBS) in civilian agencies and small business professional in the DOD. I will refer to these individuals as SBSs. Procurement Technical Assistance Center (PTAC) representatives may be used in civilian agencies and the DOD.

Every federal agency is required by law to have an Office of Small Business, and it includes the SBS personnel. The Office of Small Business is responsible for conducting outreach activities, being an advocate of small business, and supporting small business in the acquisition strategy process at a given agency. The SBS is responsible for initiating the Office of Small Business's mission. Each SBS does this by:

- Reviewing and providing input to agency acquisition strategies
- Providing guidance and counseling contractors on how to market to each agency
- Advising acquisition and program officials on small business matters

The PTAC representatives have a slightly different function. The Procurement Technical Assistance Program (PTAP) was authorized by Congress in 1985. Its intent is to increase the number of businesses capable of participating in government contracting. The PTAP is administered by the Department of Defense's Defense Logistics Agency. The PTAC program receives matching funds through cooperative agreements with state and local governments and non-profit organizations.

The PTAC representative's role is slightly different than the SBS's role because the PTAC representatives also support contractors in state and local contracting. The SBSs primarily support contractors in the federal marketplace. The PTAC representative's role in the federal, state, and local marketplace can vary from state-to-state. They do not often work with federal agencies in the development of acquisition strategies. The SBSs provide support directly to small businesses by working with the agency contracting officials in determining which contracts will be awarded to small businesses. The SBS is also a federal employee. The PTAC is not a federal employee. Even though the small business specialists and PTAC representative roles differ slightly, both help small businesses access the federal marketplace. This chapter will refer to the SBS as a result of their direct impact on small business awards at federal agencies. For more information on the role of the PTAC, visit http://www.aptac-us.org/

SMALL BUSINESS SPECIALIST'S ROLE

The SBS is an independent reviewer of proposed federal acquisitions. Their independence maximizes the support of small business participation in awards using the various small business programs including the federal government's Set-Aside Programs. They meet with the contracting officials at their agency and assist in determining which acquisitions will be set-aside for small businesses. They generally know what acquisitions are being initiated at the agency and review all new acquisitions. However, if acquisitions are being awarded via the GSA Schedule or an agency's IDIQ contracts, the SBS may not be involved in determining if an acquisition is going to be set-aside for small business. The SBS will keep all existing requirements in the Set-Aside Programs for small businesses unless he or she is unable to locate new set-aside companies to perform the work. The SBS may also move the contract out of the Set-Aside Program if the requirement itself changes in size, scope and complexity.

The SBS has a key role in helping you win government contracts. They review and provide input to government contracting officers regarding the acquisition strategy that will be used for the agency's individual acquisitions. The SBS reviews all new contract actions for their assigned agency. The SBS provides their review to the SBA representative referred to as the Procurement Center Representative (PCR). The PCR is the SBA official responsible for reviewing and signing off on an acquisition strategy for individual solicitations. They are often responsible for multiple federal agencies. As a result, they are usually not involved in the detailed discussions between the contracting officer and the SBS. They only review and approve or disapprove the final decision

95

document determining if an acquisition is placed in a SBA Set-Aside Program.

Contracting officers generally have to follow the recommendations of the SBS and PCR. In reality, the SBS and PCR essentially determine whether individual contract actions are awarded to small businesses or large businesses. The contracting officers and other program officials have to present their logic to the SBS if they want to award a contract to a company other than a small business contractor. If the SBS decides that the work should go to a small business and the contracting officer disagrees, the SBS's decision rules. The only way that a decision can be overturned is through a review from the Head of the Contracting Activity. Very few disputes of this nature take place and go to the Head of the Contracting Activity. The SBS's primary role is reviewing the acquisition strategies with the contracting and program staff.

The SBS also helps contracting officers locate small businesses that can deliver a product or perform a service. The SBSs rely on their own experiences and personal databases as well as other tools to provide advice to contracting officials. The SBS's primary tool to locate small businesses is the Dynamic Small Business Search Database (DSBS). The SBA maintains the DSBS database. When a small business registers in the SAM, they fill out a small business profile. The information provided by a small business populates the DSBS.

The DSBS is another tool contracting officers and the SBSs use to identify potential small business contractors for upcoming contracting opportunities. They research the DSBS using NAICS codes to locate small businesses for agency acquisitions. Any contractor can also use the DSBS to identify small businesses in for subcontracting, teaming and/or establishing joint ventures. The website link for the DSBS is: http://dsbs.sba.gov/dsbs/search/dsp_dsbs.cfm. If you populate the DSBS database, make sure your small business type and NAICS codes are accurate. This is a helpful tool federal officials often use to become familiar with small business companies.

The SBSs also use the FPD to help them locate government contractors. The SBSs uses the FPDS to find previously awarded contract information from all federal department and agencies. The SBS can use this site to determine if there are small businesses using NAICS codes that have performed similar work in the past. If a SBS calls your company, call them back immediately or you may be missing out on a great opportunity. You may also want to educate your staff about the SBS's role, in case they call someone in your company who is unfamiliar with their name and title.

In the previous chapters, we noted that sales staff should review the FedBizOpps notices. The SBS at each agency requires contracting officers to perform market research and post Sources Sought Notices in the FedBizOpps for new requirements. This step helps the agency determine if small business set-asides and/or small businesses are available to perform the agency's requirements, as noted in the Sources Sought Notice. If more than one set-aside small business or a small business can perform the requirement noted in the FedBizOpps posting, the SBS will require the agency to procure the requirement through a small business or small business set-aside company. Therefore, when you see Sources Sought Notices, realize that they are the result of a meeting between the SBS and the Contract Officer. These are ideal opportunities for small businesses.

97

The SBSs do not review acquisitions that are simplified dollar acquisitions (currently above $3,000 and below $150,000). The FAR mandates that all actions that are simplified acquisitions be awarded to small businesses, unless there is justification to do so otherwise. Therefore, if you are competing for acquisitions that are simplified acquisitions, know that the SBS is not involved in the decision making and selection process because all simplified actions are awarded to small business unless justified not to do so.

SMALL BUSINESS SPECIALIST'S LOCATION

The SBS's offices are often located at their individual agency for better access to the contracting officials. However, this is not always the case. The SBS may be responsible for multiple agencies and procurement offices, which means that they have to travel between those offices. This is both has its advantages and disadvantages. It is an advantage because it means that they are familiar with more than one agency, and they can provide information about multiple agencies. On the other hand, it is a disadvantage because they are spread across a few agencies/offices, and may not have as much time to get to know you or your company. You will need to be more creative in getting to know them without becoming a nuisance.

IS THE SMALL BUSINESS SPECIALIST MEETING THEIR SMALL BUSINESS GOALS?

The SBS's yearly performance appraisal is often directly tied to their ability to meet the small business goals of the agency that they support. Therefore, if you are a small business and want to win a government contract, you must find if your targeted federal agency is meeting its overall small business contracting goals. Dig a little deeper to find out which small disadvantaged business goals they are missing. If you determine that the agency you have targeted is missing the goal for a specific set-aside category, you have some options. If you are in one of the set-aside categories, then approach the agency's SBS and let them know that you are interested in helping them meet their small business goals. If you are not in one of the set-aside categories where improvement is needed, look for other businesses in that category. Propose a partnership to help the agency meet its goal. Remember, the SBSs are evaluated yearly based on the agencies they support meeting the small business goals. If you can help them achieve their goal, they will not forget you.

SMALL BUSINESS SUBCONTRACTING PLANS

The SBS also reviews and approves contractor's proposed small business subcontracting plans before a contracting officer can award a new contract. They do this to ensure that each new contract has projected small business subcontracting goals that conform to the goals of the agency they support. The subcontracting plan is incorporated into and made a material part of each new contract.

The subcontracting goals must be updated yearly by contractors. A contractor's yearly submission is forwarded by the contracting officer to the SBS for review. If the subcontracting goals are not achieved, the SBS will work with the contracting officer and contractor to try to improve the goals. In the near future, the FAR may change to create penalties, including negative past performance evaluations, if subcontracting goals are not met. Therefore, keep an eye out for FAR changes related to subcontracting plans so that you are not taken by surprise if these changes are implemented.

DEVELOP A RELATIONSHIP WITH THE SMALL BUSINESS SPECIALIST

The SBA has placed a SBS in every department and agency to support small businesses. The SBS is the key representative whose goal is to help you to win a government contract. Business development staff must learn the roles and responsibilities of the SBS at your targeted agency and personally meet the SBS. Attending the many small business conferences the SBS arranges at your targeted agency will also help you to gather information and build a relationship with the SBS. The SBS wants to help you win a government contract. If you are a small business and are awarded a government contract, you help the agency and the SBS meet their small business goals. The SBSs generally know a lot of personnel at an agency, including the contracting and program officials. They can also help you to understand how an agency functions. It is to your advantage to build a relationship with the SBS. Make sure that the SBS knows your business capabilities, skill sets, and company name. It is their job to provide you with information to make your job easier. Rely on their support services to help you gather information and build relationships. It will definitely increase your chances of receiving an award of a federal government contract.

CHAPTER 10

ATTEND AGENCY CONFERENCES

Another great way to gain knowledge, gather information, and even develop relationships is to attend agency conferences. Your targeted agency may hold various forms of acquisition conferences at various times of the year. Agencies in general are very inconsistent regarding the scheduling of the conferences. Therefore, do not be surprised if your targeted agency does not have an acquisition conference in a fiscal year. The conferences purpose, time, and dates are generally posted on an agency's website or the FedBizOpps. In general, agency conferences are a great place to learn about upcoming solicitations, learn about agency programs and meet both industry and government officials. In this chapter, I will describe various types of agency conferences that every contractor should consider attending to help you gain knowledge, gather information, and develop relationships about your targeted agency.

SMALL BUSINESS CONFERENCES

The agency's SBS is often responsible for organizing and holding conferences that support small businesses. The conferences are also often valuable to large businesses. These conferences are held at an agency to educate small businesses about what it buys and how it buys its products and services. The conferences also provide introductions of senior level program office and contracting office officials. These small business conferences often include matchmaking events that allow small and large businesses the opportunity to meet each other. These matchmaking events are often held with contractors who already perform work at an agency. You should contact the SBS at your targeted agency to find out when a small business conference is being held.

GENERAL INFORMATION CONFERENCES

Some agencies have conferences for new contractors that provide general information about how an agency is structured and functions. The conference will give an overview of major programs and describe how an agency buys its product and services. During the conference, there will be introductions of key officials from various programs within an agency. The conference does not often go into detail regarding the agency's programs and upcoming acquisitions. However, it provides a general overview of the agency. Many experienced sales staff considers these conferences to be a waste of time, since they do not go into great detail regarding upcoming procurements. These conferences are generally best for the new uninformed contractors that know little about an agency. However, it is still a good networking event even for experienced contractors.

INDIVIDUAL PROGRAM CONFERENCES

A conference may provide detailed information of individual programs at an agency. These conferences are generally for large and small businesses. The agency sponsoring the conference will describe the technical aspects of each program, introduce the key agency officials responsible for the program, and describe where they see the program in the future. They may also discuss future procurements. These smaller conferences are a good way to meet the other contractor personnel with similar skill sets and learn about the competition. The conference will also provide the opportunity to judge the level of interest in a particular agency program. The conferences are valuable because they provide specific information regarding an agency's programs that you may be targeting.

PREPROPOSAL CONFERENCES

Agencies also have preproposal conferences to discuss upcoming agency solicitations. The conference locations and times are posted in the FedBizOpps and are held in response to an active solicitation. They are often held after the release of a solicitation, but before the proposal due date. The purpose of a preproposal conference is to help contractors understand the particular requirements and proposal instructions for an active solicitation. If the agency holds a conference about a procurement that has been set-aside for a small businesses, large businesses often attend to gather information and develop additional contacts.

You must attend these meetings if you want to propose on a particular procurement as a prime or subcontractor. Many small businesses attend the meetings to locate and leverage large businesses with a proven track record. If you are a small business and the preproposal conference requirement offered is similar to your products and services, you must attend the meeting. These meeting can be used to gather information, regardless whether you are a large or small business or whether you intend to submit a proposal on a solicitation. Therefore, go to a preproposal conference with the intent of meeting the competition and developing relationships with contractors you can partner with on the solicitation. You may also be able to gain information and develop relationships regarding future procurements.

DEPARTMENT LEVEL CONFERENCES

Federal government departments may also hold conferences to review how the whole department functions, and introduce the SBSs from each agency. These conferences are generally for small business contractors. Departments hold conferences to familiarize small businesses with the various roles and responsibilities of individual agencies in a department. The meetings also introduce the SBSs or PTAC representatives from each agency in the department. For example, if the HHS holds a small business conference at its headquarters in Washington D.C., it would ideally have in attendance the SBSs from all eleven operating divisions/agencies. This would include representatives from the Centers for Medicare and Medicaid Services, the National Institute of Health, and the Centers for Disease Control, among others. These meeting are good to attend if you are just starting to do business with a particular department or if you are a new small business.

CONFERENCES TO MEET AGENCY REPRESENTATIVES

Agencies also invite contractors to their offices on "meet and greet" industry days. These conferences usually include a specific group of contractors, similar small business contractors, information technology contractors, security contractors, etc. The contractors in attendance are located behind tables in a large conference room. These meetings give the federal officials a chance to learn about the contractors' capabilities, work experience, and how their products and services can be procured in an efficient and effective manner. These conferences do not work if the agency officials do not attend. The agency officials may be busy with a full agenda of meetings and do not always take the time to attend these conferences. They may also think that they already know all of the "real" contractors, and refuse to attend. Therefore, these conferences may not be worth participating in unless the appropriate personnel attend the conference.

MATCH MAKING CONFERENCES

Agencies can also stage meetings to help large businesses find small businesses. These meeting help the large companies by providing small business contacts, and also help the small businesses locate large businesses at their targeted agency. The conferences are a win-win situation for both large and small businesses. If you are a small business, you should ask your agency's SBS if they have scheduled meetings similar to these conferences. If they do, you should attend these meetings. You can potentially meet dozens of large businesses over the course of one day, instead of waiting the months it would take to schedule personal meetings at the large business contractor locations. It will also help you learn the key contractors at the agency, and give you a start in establishing relationships.

PRECAUTION: IF YOU SIGN UP, YOU MUST ATTEND

If you do sign up for these meetings, make sure that you show up. If you are a no-show, you may be placed on the waiting list the next time your targeted agency has a conference. If you cannot attend, notify the agency that you cannot attend well in advance so that the agency can make room for another contractor. If you do not, it may place a black eye on the reputation of your company. Attending agency conferences will lead to you to having a better opportunity to gain knowledge, gather information, and building relationships.

CHAPTER 11

YOU MUST KNOW FAR 15.201

GOVERNMENT AND CONTRACTOR STAFF ARE UNINFORMED

Sales staff and program managers always want to meet in-person with agency officials. However, very few contractor personnel that I have met through the years understand the rules regarding when you can meet with them. For that matter, very few government personnel understand the rules regarding when you can meet with contractor personnel. It is vitally important to understand the rules and regulations in order to increase your chances of meeting with agency officials. One of the biggest frustrations of my thirty-two year government career was attempting to make both government and contractor personnel to understand the rules and regulations regarding when government personnel can have exchanges with contractor personnel.

I have presented at large industry conferences with hundreds of experienced contractor business development personnel in the audience. While presenting, I would often ask the audience, "How many people in the audience know the language contained in FAR 15.201?" Of the three to four hundred people in the audience, only three or four hands would be raised. In addition to conferences, I have had individual meetings with hundreds of contractor personnel. I always ask each contractor, "Do you know FAR 15.201?" Very rarely do I find a business development representative or capture consultant that knows this FAR clause. As was stated in the first chapter of the book, one of the three cornerstones of marketing and selling to the

107

government is gaining knowledge. FAR 15.201 is one clause in which you must understand to increase your chances of receiving a government contract.

THE MOST IMPORTANT CLAUSE FOR SALES STAFF

FAR 15.201, "Exchanges with Industry before the Receipt of Proposals" is the most important clause in the FAR for sales staff. This FAR clause is important because it will assist sales staff to gather information and build relationships with agency personnel. This FAR clause is also a key clause that industry officials can use to educate government staff. It will help to build bridges and open doors for government contractors. It is therefore vitally important to the wellbeing of our country that this FAR clause is taught to government acquisition officials. This FAR clause provides industry representatives the leverage to encourage federal officials to interact with them.

Most of my government and contractor contacts are unfamiliar with the FAR 15.201 and some very experienced business development and capture staff do not know that it even exists. Federal officials generally do not know if and when they can meet with contractor personnel, and are therefore hesitant to do so. It is easier for government officials to avoid contractor personnel than consider if they are allowed to talk to them.

Contractor personnel share the blame as they do not know this FAR clause or understand how it will increase their ability to engage government officials. I have met with hundreds of sales staff to discuss their products, services and capabilities. Why? I meet with them because I understand the value and intent of this clause. Very few sales staff is knowledgeable of the language contained in the FAR clause and I have had to educate them in regards to it.

FAR 15.201

I have included the language in FAR 15.201 because of its importance to your government contracting journey. FAR 15.201 states:

15.201 Exchanges with industry before receipt of proposals.

(a) Exchanges of information among all interested parties, from the earliest identification of a requirement through receipt of proposals, are encouraged. Any exchange of information must be consistent with procurement integrity requirements (see 3.104). Interested parties include potential offerors, end users, Government acquisition and supporting personnel, and others involved in the conduct or outcome of the acquisition.

(b) The purpose of exchanging information is to improve the understanding of Government requirements and industry capabilities, thereby allowing potential offerors to judge whether or how they can satisfy the Government's requirements, and enhancing the Government's ability to obtain quality supplies and services, including construction, at reasonable prices, and increase efficiency in proposal preparation, proposal evaluation, negotiation, and contract award.

(c) Agencies are encouraged to promote early exchanges of information about future acquisitions. An early exchange of information among industry and the program manager, contracting officer, and other participants in the acquisition process can identify and resolve concerns regarding the acquisition strategy, including proposed contract type, terms and conditions, and acquisition planning schedules; the feasibility of the requirement, including performance requirements, statements of work, and data requirements; the suitability of the proposal instructions and evaluation criteria, including the approach for assessing past performance information; the availability of reference documents; and any other industry concerns or questions. Some techniques to promote early exchanges of information are—

(1) Industry or small business conferences;

(2) Public hearings;

(3) Market research, as described in Part 10;

(4) One-on-one meetings with potential offerors (any that are substantially involved with potential contract terms and conditions should include the contracting officer; also see paragraph (f) of this section regarding restrictions on disclosure of information);

(5) Presolicitation notices;

(6) Draft RFPs;

(7) RFIs;

(8) Presolicitation or preproposal conferences; and

(9) Site visits.

PAST LANGUAGE

The FAR language regarding exchanges with industry representatives changed in 1994. Prior to that timeframe, the language contained in the FAR did not allow agency officials to talk to industry representatives when the agency became aware of a need to procure a product or service. If it was discovered that a contracting official had discussed a known requirement with industry representatives, it led to Procurement Integrity Violations, which were punishable with a possible prison sentence.

Contracting officials were prohibited from conducting these discussions until late 1994. Prior to 1994, government officials were very limited in their ability to have exchanges with industry representatives when they identified the need to procure a product or service.

CHANGED LANGUAGE

The 1994 FAR change was a 180-degree change in direction from the previous language. The current FAR 15.201 language provides industry personnel the exact ammunition they needed to talk to and gain access to agency representatives. However, no one in industry or the government seems to know that it exists. If federal contractors educated themselves regarding the value of this clause, it could pass this knowledge to the government representatives. The government acquisition officials talk a good game regarding wanting to save money and make the government more efficient and effective. This can be accomplished by engaging industry regarding the latest and greatest industry technologies and innovations. This clause "encourages" these discussions; however, I have met industry representative after industry representative who cannot gain access to federal officials, or teach them about new technologies and innovations.

One of my acquaintances called me a few years back to let me know that his employer, a large IT company could save an agency thousands of dollars with new technology and a new pricing methodology. The contractor already had established contracts with the agency. He had talked to his government program official, who told him to call another senior acquisition official at that particular agency. None of the acquisition officials had provided easy access to him or other industry officials. He told me that the agency acquisition official was not interested in hearing him deliver his sales pitch. At the time, the President of the

111

U.S. was asking each federal agency to reduce its spending by 10% each year. That agency needed to find some savings, but they still would not talk to the company representative about saving money.

Many sales staff have the same problem trying to gain access to government officials. The FAR 15.201 intent was to change that by encouraging government officials to talk to industry representatives. The meetings described in the FAR 15.201 do not happen as often as they should. The meetings are often restricted to the same old vendors who already have access to the government facilities.

A SUCCESS STORY

I personally used this clause in the year 2000 to help my agency award the largest IT contract it had in existence prior to that point in time. In 1999, prior to Y2K, my agency had some large email system meltdowns. At that point in time, there were many contractors managing various pieces of the IT infrastructure. When the email system failed for a few days, the Chief Information Officer gathered more than fifty contractors into a room to ascertain what went wrong. They all pointed their fingers at one another, and no one took responsibility or fixed the problem. As a result of this crisis, the agency decided to have one contractor manage the entire infrastructure. I was the contracting officer for the effort.

I was very knowledgeable about acquisition strategies, but did not know the best way to go about this particular acquisition. Understanding the value of the FAR 15.201, I proceeded to schedule meetings with a lot of personnel in the industry to engage in discussions regarding the acquisition strategy, contract type, availability of performance metrics, proposal instructions, and evaluation criteria. In addition, I had discussions with other federal agencies to gain additional knowledge of their best

112

practices. I also had discussions with the Gartner Group, an organization that advises the government in all areas of information technology.

The discussions with industry representatives primarily shaped the overall structure of the solicitation and acquisition. Another agency's IDIQ contract was used to reduce the risk of a Post-Award Protest, and my agency only had to pay a minimal fee for using it. I decided to use a fixed-price task order for the effort. A fixed price task order had never been used at my agency for such a large IT effort. I also initiated a two-step selection process to eliminate unqualified vendors early in the solicitation process. This resulted in savings to industry by eliminating contractors early in process. It also resulted in savings to the government by reducing the number of proposals that were reviewed in the second phase of the solicitation.

Contractors that passed Step One were each awarded a fixed price task order that required the contractors to submit a contract deliverable describing the configuration of the agency's IT infrastructure in five years into the future. The deliverable became government property and an evaluation factor of the solicitation. There were four full days of due diligent meetings to help new contractors fully understand the agency's IT infrastructure. These solicitation/acquisition techniques were discovered and used as a result of conversations with industry representatives and officials from other agencies. The contract award was made on schedule and resulted in significant savings to the government. A contractor that had not previously had any contracts with the agency received this large award.

The unique procurement strategies were not mine. I gained the best practice information from industry representatives and other government agency officials. In fact, industry representatives told me the other agencies and government personnel to contact. This task order was a very successful endeavor for my agency, and one of the largest reasons for that success was my engagement with industry representatives.

I am a staunch supporter of using the intent of the FAR 15.201 to help the government procure its products and services in an effective and efficient manner. My experience on the procurement described above changed my perception of what industry can do to help the government acquisition officials. If industry did not share its best practices with me on this procurement, the acquisition would have had very different results, and may not have been as successful.

MYTH BUSTERS

I have been preaching the virtue of the FAR 15.201 for over a decade. Much to my surprise on February 2, 2011, Daniel Gordon, the Administrator of the Office of Federal Procurement Policy (OFPP), issued a memo titled "Myth-Busting": Addressing Misconceptions to Improve Communication with Industry during the Acquisition Process." The memo stated:

> The Federal Acquisition Regulation (FAR) authorizes a broad range of opportunities for vendor communication, but agencies often do not take full advantage of these existing flexibilities. Some agency officials may be reluctant to engage in these exchanges out of fear of protests or fear of binding the agency in an unauthorized manner; others may be unaware of effective strategies that can help the acquisition workforce and industry make the best use of their time and resources. Similarly, industry may be concerned that talking with an agency may create a conflict of interest that will preclude them from competing on

114

future requirements, or industry may be apprehensive about engaging in meaningful conversations in the presence of other vendors.

Locate the Myth Busting Memo February 2, 2011 on the internet to learn more about the Administrator of OFPP's position. Once you read the OFPP Memo, you will understand as is stated in the FAR 15.201 that "exchanges with industry is encouraged." Learn and use the FAR 15.201 to your advantage in the marketplace. Educate the agency officials about the language. It will go a long way to making the government's acquisitions and contracts more efficient and effective. This knowledge will also give you an edge on the competition.

IT IS NOT AS HARD AS YOU THINK

In 2012, a contracting officer representative requested that we interview an 8(a) contractor as a result of a new requirement that had to be awarded in Fiscal Year 2012. I was unfamiliar with the contractor, but called the contractor and scheduled the meeting. I asked the contracting officer representative where she got the contractor's name and she said she knew nothing about the contractor, but had received an email from him in which he described his company's capabilities.

Upon arrival, I asked the contractor to provide a background about his company. He told me that he owned a commercial money mailer/advertising company for over a decade. The recession in 2008 caused his company's revenue to decrease substantially. A friend had told him that he could become a small and disadvantaged minority business and pursue government contracting opportunities. He received his 8(a) status from the federal government in late 2011. By the time I met this individual, he already had three government contract awards.

I asked him how he received his contract awards so fast with no experience. He told me that he crafted an email that included his company's capabilities and the FAR 15.201. The email was sent to government officials. The email told the government officials that the FAR 15.201 encourages the federal government officials to talk to contractors. He stated that he was very successful using this strategy. He also told me that other contractors he knew were reluctant to do this because they did not want to make the government officials mad. However, he used a strategy that was perfectly legal and resulted in his government contracting business flourishing in a short period of time.

Use the FAR 15.201 to gain access to government officials. Develop the knowledge to educate government staff about what is stated in the FAR 15.201. If you gain knowledge about this clause, it will help you build relationships with government staff. In doing so, your gained knowledge will go a long way in helping you win a government contract.

CHAPTER 12

HOW & WHEN TO MEET WITH AGENCY STAFF: THE GOLDEN FOUR

GAINING ACCESS

Now that you know the meaning and intent of the language contained in the FAR 15.201, you are moving in the right direction to gain access to the agency officials. Gaining access to the federal officials may be the hardest endeavor for your organization. It is one of the biggest challenges contractors face year after year. Through my years of government contracting, I have developed the Brian Hebbel Golden Four, tried and true meeting strategies that will give you the best chance to gaining access to federal officials. Three of the Golden Four meeting strategies are commonly used. The fourth strategy will become important in the next few years and I will explain why in this chapter. These four strategies should always be discussed with your management team prior to contacting federal officials. The Golden Four will result in a win-win strategy for both your company and federal officials. The Golden Four strategies that will assist sales staff to gain access to federal officials include:

- Save money
- Solve a problem
- New technology
- Acquisition Strategies

I have observed each strategy being utilized by contractors throughout my 32 year career. It is important for you to know and always remember these strategies in order to be successful in the federal marketplace. Therefore, I will explain the Golden Four strategies in a

117

very succinct and easy to remember manner. My experience has shown that if you want to gain access to federal officials, you have to bring a key ingredient to the table that will benefit them. By helping federal officials to save money, solve a problem, provide updates regarding new technologies or discuss future acquisition strategies, you will help them to identify opportunities for improvement at their agency. In addition, these strategies will help make your targeted agency more efficient and effective. Remember however that most federal officials do not realize how you can help them or know what the rules are regarding discussions with contractors. Therefore, you will need to educate the officials regarding the FAR 15.201 and then discuss one or more of the Golden Four techniques. Overall, this will increase your chances of gaining access to your targeted agency.

I attended a conference and an Agency Chief Information Officer told the attending contractors that he would not meet with contractors to discuss their corporate capabilities. He stated he would only meet with contractors if they could help the agency solve a problem. In general, do not try to schedule meetings with agency officials to discuss your corporate capabilities. There are probably thousands of companies in the marketplace similar to your company. Agency officials do not have time to meet with every contractor to review their corporate capabilities. However, if you can help the agency save money, solve a problem, provide updates regarding new technologies, or discuss future acquisition strategies, they are more likely to remember your company.

GOLDEN RULE #1: SAVE MONEY

Federal agencies have faced significant budget reductions in recent years. The recent budget sequestration cuts resulted in automatic spending reductions to many federal agencies. As a result, federal agencies are looking for creative ways to accomplish their mission with reduced budgets. If your company has solutions to save the government money, it may help you to win a government contract and build your company's name recognition. If your company has software tools that could save the government money, it may also help you to win a government contract and build your company's name recognition. I have read problems and solutions to government budget issues in the Office of Inspector General reports, Congressional inquiries, newspapers, magazines, and even emails. Saving money is one of the constant issues facing a federal agency. Prior to calling the federal officials for a meeting, you should develop creative ways to help the federal officials save money. If you do, they are more likely to meet with you.

GOLDEN RULE #2: SOLVE A PROBLEM

Federal agencies face difficult challenges implementing new programs in short timeframes. They are always looking for ways to make their programs function more effectively and efficiently. Agency's problems are opportunities for improvement. Therefore, if you know that an agency is having problems, it is to your advantage to present solutions using your company's tools and/or skill sets. Problems agencies face are often found in the Office of Inspector General reports, Congressional inquiries, newspapers, magazines and even emails. Solving problems is a constant issue facing all federal agencies. Prior to calling the federal officials for a meeting, think of creative ways to help the federal officials solve an agency problem. If you do, then they will be more likely to meet with you.

GOLDEN RULE #3: NEW TECHNOLOGY

Technology is changing faster and faster with each passing day. In the past 50 years, the changes we have

119

seen are mind-blowing. Computer memory is doubling every 18 months to 2 years. The Human Genome Project is going to identify and map all of the genes of the human body. Many fields of science are drastically changing as a result of new technology. New technologies are also driving changes in federal agencies. The rapid advances in technology have made it difficult for government agencies to keep up with the changing innovations.

If your company is marketing and selling the latest technology in your field, the government officials will want to hear from you regarding what new technology is being used and sold in the marketplace. New technology creates an opportunity for you to gain access to federal officials. Prior to calling the federal officials for a meeting, think how you can reach them by educating them about new technology that may impact their agency. If you do, then they will be more likely to meet with you.

GOLDEN RULE #4: DISCUSS ACQUISITION STRATEGIES

Believe it or not, agencies can use help from contractors to develop acquisition strategies. If you want to meet with agency officials, discussing the acquisition strategy for future procurements is one way to do it. Generally, it is an unusual step for an agency official to engage contractors to discuss future acquisition strategies. It does not happen often, however this is going to change over the next few years, particularly in Civilian Agencies. I will explain why in the proceeding paragraphs.

If you are going to meet with agency officials to discuss acquisition strategies, I would advise that you do it very early in the acquisition planning cycle of an agency Program. Agencies should develop acquisition strategies months before a solicitation is released and competed. In fact, they really need to know the acquisition strategy prior

120

to writing a statement of work. The acquisition strategy and/or contract type could change based on how a statement of work is written. Acquisition strategies are usually completed by agency officials early in the acquisition cycle. You need to meet with acquisition officials six months to two years before the solicitation is released for competition. If you do not do plan on meeting with agency officials early in the acquisition process, the agency officials will not want to meet with you because their strategy is probably already developed.

You can help the agency officials formulate the acquisition in many areas including the acquisition strategy, proposed contract type, terms and conditions, performance requirements, statement of work, data requirements, proposal instructions, and evaluation criteria to name a few. This can be accomplished by expressing to agency officials your opinion, giving suggestions or providing general information even though you have not seen or know the agency's acquisition strategy.

Golden Rule #4, "Discussing Acquisition Strategies" will be a more often used technique in the upcoming years. This technique will be popular in future years because Civilian Agencies are now required to officially designate Program Managers and Project Managers. This will occur as a result of the "Office of Federal Procurement Policy's October 2009 Acquisition Development Workforce Strategic Plan for Civilian Agencies." The 2009 policy recommends improvements in the acquisition workforce by strengthening and formally implementing the roles of Project Manager and Program Manager. In 2015, a new formal training curriculum is being required for senior program officials who will be responsible for their particular programs. The Federal Acquisition Institute

(FAI), the federal organization responsible for providing a curriculum and training to the acquisition workforce, states on their website that their mission is to "promote acquisition workforce excellence though ... Professional Certification Training." The FAI website states that "Program Managers and Project Managers (P/PMs) are critical in developing accurate government requirements, defining measureable performance standards, and managing life-cycle activities to insure that intended outcomes are achieved."

The designated Program Managers for an agency must now go through a series of training courses to improve their acquisition competencies. Included in their new role is the responsibility to develop a written acquisition strategy and acquisition plan for their specific programs. They may or will need other government officials and industry representatives to assist in the development of their acquisition strategy and acquisition plan and formalize the document. These new roles and requirements of the Program Manager and Project Manager create your opportunity to assist them in developing the acquisition strategy.

However, you must be cautious. There are strict conflict of interest rules that could prohibit you from submitting a proposal if you helped to develop the government solicitation documents or had access to information that was not provided to other contractors. You need to ensure that these discussions do not violate any conflict of interest rules.

OTHER TECHNIQUES TO MEET WITH AGENCY STAFF

There are other techniques that you can use to help you meet with agency staff beside the Golden Four Rules. They include the techniques described in various chapters in this book. Some of the key techniques may include hiring someone who personally knows the federal officials, market your company's distinctions, acquire a badge that enables you access to the federal buildings or rely on your technical staff that are on-site. There are a lot of ways to meet with agency staff. However, in most cases, you may be better able to deliver a presentation if you use one of the Golden Four techniques.

TEAM WITH OTHER CONTRACTORS

If you want to help agency officials save money, solve a problem, learn about new technologies in the marketplace, or learn about potential acquisition strategies, I would recommend that you consider teaming with other contractors when meetings with agency officials. Depending on the issue, leveraging your partners in the marketplace may help to convince an agency official to meet with you. By having more than one contractor in attendance, the agency official may be more apt to meet with industry representatives. The agency official will understand the industry representatives' commitment to the issue to be discussed and therefore agree to meet. The official can meet four contractors in one meeting and learn about new technology rather than having four separate meetings. For example, you may be able to solve an agency problem and a teaming partner may have a business relationship with an agency official. In this scenario, teaming together will result in a benefit to all parties. Think outside of the box and use your industry contacts to leverage meetings with agency officials. By using other contractors, you are more likely to secure meetings at your targeted agency.

YOUR BUSINESS CARD IS A VALUABLE TOOL

I have a final tip to convey regarding meeting with agency officials. When you meet with agency officials, your business card is one of the most important informational tools. It is small, easy to handle, and should contain valuable information. If designed and arranged properly, it will be an easy way for the intended recipient to remember you. The best business card that I have seen was a double-sided business card with the following information:

- Company logo
- Company name
- Name of official
- Phone number
- Email address
- NAICS Codes
- Small business size status (8(a), Women-Owned Business, etc.)
- Core business functions (eight were listed)

The business card contained a lot of information that is valuable to federal officials. Particularly important was the small business size status, NAICS codes, and the core functions. Most business cards that I have seen do not contain all three of these elements. SBSs and other contracting officials can use this small business card as a memory jogger of your corporation. This information may make the difference in your company being remembered or forgotten.

MEETING GOVERNMENT PURCHASE CARDS HOLDERS

If you are receiving government awards through an agency's government Purchase Card Program (credit card program), or want to do so in the future, you need to be acquainted with the government staff making the credit card purchases and educate them about your company. Federal agencies often use the government Purchase Card to buy agency products and services. In accordance with the FAR, cardholders may use their government Purchase Card for purchases totaling less than the micro purchase threshold ($3,000 in 2015). If the cardholder is a warranted contracting officer, in accordance with the FAR, the cardholder may purchase goods and services worth up to $150,000, the simplified purchase threshold. In February 2015, there was discussion to raise the simplified purchase threshold to $500,000. Generally, all purchases between the micro-purchase level and $150,000 are reserved for competition among small businesses.

The information regarding Purchase Card buys above the micro purchase threshold are placed in the FPDS. As a result, you can find the contracting officer responsible for making Purchase Card awards. If you want to receive Purchase Card awards at your targeted agency, you should make every effort to become familiar with the contracting officer(s) responsible for making the purchase card awards. If the award is less than $3,000, any Purchase Card official at the agency can make an award. It is your job to know who they are and get acquainted with them.

Meeting with agency staff may be your biggest challenge in federal contracting. I challenge each of you to explore the value of the FAR 15.201. Start educating the government contracting and industry officials regarding this clause. Your individual efforts will help to break down the barriers between contractors and the government. You must have the personnel on your staff that knows how to gain access to the right federal officials. If your company does not develop techniques for meeting with federal staff, it will be hard to develop relationships with them. If you do not develop relationships with agency staff, your goal of winning a federal contract may be far more difficult than you anticipated. Meeting with agency staff is a key technique to help you win a government contract.

The Golden Four are great strategies to help gain access to federal officials. Using the Golden Four techniques will result in a winning strategy for your company. Use them to your advantage because they are crucial techniques that must be included in your toolbox to be successful in the federal marketplace.

CHAPTER 13

EDUCATE AGENCY STAFF

It is extremely important for sales staff to understand the need to educate agency staff regarding how to award your company a contract in an efficient and effective manner. Sales staff needs to educate federal officials about your company's size status and the resulting benefits afforded to your company. They also need to educate federal officials about the Government-Wide Acquisition Contracts (GWAC) or agency IDIQ contracts your company has available in the federal marketplace and how contract awards can be made in an efficient and effective manner using these contracting vehicles. It is an important sales practice that must be considered at every sales meeting with a government official. I do not know any business development or capture staff that uses this technique on a consistent basis. In fact, sales staff rarely utilize this technique. In this chapter, I will explain the use and importance of this sales technique.

EDUCATING FEDERAL STAFF IS AN ESSENTIAL SALES TECHNIQUE

Sales staff must educate federal officials how to buy their products and services in an effective and efficient manner. This sales technique seems odd to most government sales staff. When the sales staff is meeting with government officials, they think they are talking to government officials who know all of the government acquisition strategies and procurement techniques. The government personnel must know how to buy products and services using all of the contracting vehicles that are

127

available in the federal marketplace. Do you think this is true?

In reality, there are so many federal government contracting vehicles in place today; no one contracting officer will use them all. Each one has so many different rules, regulations, and ordering procedures. In fact, not one government official including experienced contracting officials knows how to award contracts and task orders using all of them. If you can tactfully educate the contracting and program officials regarding the federal contracts that you have available and that you are authorized to use at your targeted agency, you will have a leg-up on your competition.

EDUCATE AGENCY OFFICIALS ABOUT YOUR INDEFINITE DELIVERY INDEFINITE QUANTITY CONTRACTS

Since the late 1990s, there has been a proliferation of individual agency IDIQ contracts and GWACs that can be used by all federal agencies. The proliferation of the IDIQ contracts has created confusion in the federal marketplace for contractors and federal officials. Contractors are confused because they are unsure which contracting strategies and vehicles individual agencies or contracting officers tend to use. Federal officials are confused because they are unfamiliar with all of the contracting vehicles available at their own agency and throughout the federal government. However, IDIQ contracting strategies are not going away anytime soon.

The General Services Administration (GSA) GWAC schedule contracts are the most popular federal government IDIQ contracts. However, some agencies have their own IDIQ contracts. An IDIQ contract is intended to provide an agency with a pool of contractors, whose contract terms and conditions have already been

128

negotiated. If authorized by the Economy Act, other agencies can use an agency's IDIQ contract. IDIQ contracts enable agencies to buy products and services in an efficient and effective manner. However, there are so many IDIQ contracts in the federal marketplace today that few contracting officials actually know all of the IDIQ's in existence or how to use them. Therefore, it is very important for your sales staff to know the ordering procedures of your company's federal contracts, including your IDIQ contracts. Furthermore, you must educate the federal contracting and program officials regarding how to use your IDIQ contracts.

If an agency has IDIQ contracts in place, they may not be using the GSA Schedule or any other agency's GWACs. If the agency buys products and services similar to what you sell, and you are not on their IDIQ contract, the agency contracting officials may not be able to deviate from using their IDIQ contract. Therefore, the door could be closed to selling products or services to your targeted agency. If this is the situation, you may be wasting your time educating them about your IDIQ contracts. Regardless, IDIQ contracts role in the federal acquisition process has created some confusion in the federal marketplace. Therefore, you need to help eliminate some of the confusion by educating the agency staff.

RULES AND REGULATIONS OFTEN CHANGE

Federal acquisition rules and regulations often change. As they change, your job is to educate the federal staff regarding what the changes mean to them. Rule and regulation changes may impact not only how products and services are procured on IDIQ contracts, but may also impact how they are procured on all contracts throughout the federal government. For instance, in 2011, the SBA changed the rules and regulations used for competing

Service-Disabled Veteran-Owned Businesses and Small Women-Owned Businesses. Many contractor officials did not understand how individual agencies would react to these FAR changes.

Contractor personnel can use any FAR changes to their advantage by discussing and educating the impact of the changes with agency contracting and program officials. Your job is to let the agency officials know what the changes mean to your business and to them. It may take agency personnel months or even years to determine what the changes mean to them. The majority of your education will be in the ordering processes and procedures for your contract vehicles. However, you may need to educate the federal contracting and program staff in a lot of other areas including acquisition strategies and techniques. If you can help them maneuver through and understand the impact of changes to various rules and regulations, they will remember your company in the future.

ASSUME THEY DO NOT KNOW

When you meet with federal staff, always start with presuming that they are unfamiliar with the ordering processes and procedures of your federal contracts. Presume that they have not procured products and services using all of the SBA's Disadvantaged Business Set-Aside Programs. Imagine that they have not used creative acquisition strategies that are used at other agencies. Think that the federal individual program personnel, contract specialists, and contracting officers may not know their own internal IDIQ contracts, or those in place at other agencies. Assume that the program and contracting officials have never purchased products and services using the GSA Schedules or other agencies' IDIQ contracting vehicles. Start from scratch in regards to educating these officials when pitching your own products and services.

CORS DO NOT KNOW

Sales staffs have a lot of discussions with contracting officer representatives (COR), who administer the technical aspects of a contract after the award. Most CORs perform pre-award contracting activities for only a short period of time. Their managers may know slightly more about various acquisition techniques, but they have a very limited understanding of the contracting vehicles and strategies that exist in the federal marketplace. If you are dealing with CORs and other program officials, presume that they are unfamiliar with the acquisition contracting vehicles and techniques that are available to your company. Therefore, it is your job to educate them regarding your federal contracts and the contract's ordering procedures.

A COR may also have very limited knowledge about the steps necessary to buy your products and services, even if you have existing government contracts. Most sales staff assume that the COR and senior program officials have equal knowledge of federal contracting vehicles and acquisition processes. However, they do not have equal knowledge. CORs are generally less knowledgeable than senior program officials. You need to educate both of them about your contracting vehicles and how to efficiently and effectively procure your products and services. Your job is to make their job easier and motivate them to procure your products and services. Educating CORs and program officials is a good start to building a solid relationship.

131

EXPERIENCED CONTRACTING OFFICERS MAY NOT KNOW

Federal contracting officers and contract specialists are more astute than CORs regarding the techniques used to buy products and services for the federal government. They receive more acquisition training and education as compared to CORs. On-the-job training also provides them with various types of acquisitions to broaden their experience. Very few contracting officers and contract specialists buy products and services using all of the various GWACs, GSA Schedules, agency IDIQs, and small business set-aside acquisitions available to them. Their workload does not give them the opportunity to procure products and services using all of the various contracting vehicles in the federal marketplace. When you meet with them, presume that they do not know how to use the various GSA contracting vehicles or other agency GWACs. Additionally, presume that they do not know the acquisition procedures for each of the Small Disadvantaged Business Set-Aside Programs. Presume that they are also unfamiliar with their own agency IDIQ contracts. Your job is to educate them how to use the contracting vehicles available to your company.

DO NOT RUFFLE FEATHERS, BE GENTLE

When you educate the government contracting and program officials, you need to have the right sales staff in place, and make sure that they have good people skills. The right skill set includes the salesperson's ability to quickly determine the knowledge base of the government officials without insulting their intelligence and have the knowledge to explain how to use your company's contracting vehicles. The sales staff should also be able to adequately explain how to use your acquisition vehicles in a clear manner. Additionally, they must determine how

132

knowledgeable the government officials are regarding the use of other acquisition techniques. If the sales staff appears to be condescending to the federal contracting or programming officials, it can result in permanent damage in their ability to meet with these officials in the future. However, if you size up the situation and provide the needed education to the contracting and program staff, you can build relationships with government officials.

SALES STAFF NEED TO BE EDUCATED

You must ensure that your sales staff is fully educated regarding the federal government's acquisition process and your company's contracting vehicles. If they are not, the federal contracting officials may quickly dismiss your company or your company may be missing an acquisition opportunity. Sales staffs are often not as educated as they should be regarding various federal acquisition techniques. For instance, most sales staff that I have encountered are not familiar with the difference in the ordering procedures of the GSA Schedule when the requirement has a statement of work or does not have a statement of work. There are big differences in these two ordering processes that your sales staff must know and understand (see FAR 8.405-1 & 2). If your sales staff are not adequately trained, send them to courses similar to those attended by government staff. If they are not knowledgeable regarding the various federal acquisition contracts available to your company and the ordering procedures, they cannot educate the government personnel. Successfully trained sales staff can increase your company's sales goals faster than you may have imagined.

EDUCATING AGENCY STAFF IS WORTHWHILE

If you are fully aware of this education concept when you talk to the government officials, you can make your meetings more meaningful, helpful, and worthwhile for you and the federal officials. The contracting official's job is to buy products and services in an efficient and effective manner. If you can help them do this, you will become a valued partner in the acquisition process. The FAR 15.201 encourages the exchange of information with the acquisition staff and visa-versa. The exchange of information includes helping contracting staff understand the various contracting vehicles that are in the massive federal marketplace. Always include this concept in your marketing and sales plan. If you can educate federal officials regarding the contracting vehicles that you have in place, it may result in more opportunities for your company to receive a government contract award.

CHAPTER 14

MARKET WHAT MAKES YOUR COMPANY DISTINCT

Now that you know that the FAR encourages the exchange of information with federal officials, start meeting with federal staff. When you meet with federal staff, there is another marketing technique you should also consider. Specifically, consider marketing the distinct advantages your company has in the federal marketplace. In any relationship, you have to bring something of value to the table. In your relationship with the many government officials that you may meet, you need to propose something of value to entice them to meet with you. Remember, it is not always about you. It is about what you can do for them. Bringing something of value to the table increases your odds of meeting with them. Your company's distinctions in the federal marketplace can provide this value.

When considering your company's distinctions, compare every aspect of your company's products and services to your competitors. Any differentiators will give you the ability to market your company to the government. Distinctions can be in the form of technical advantages and/or unique pricing approaches. For example, consider the following questions: Will the release of a new product result in reduced maintenance charges? Do your company's new servers use less electricity than any other servers in the marketplace? Will your company's new database help the agency collect data that was not previously collected? Draw up a list of advantages for your company's products and services and outline how they will help the government before you meet with the federal officials.

Most sales representatives sell to the federal government with the understanding and belief that their products and services have distinct advantages in the marketplace. If the products and services do not have advantages, then they will be difficult to market. If you are a sales representative, you already know what advantages your company's products and services hold. These advantages need to be marketed to your targeted agency.

HELP THE PROGRAM OFFICIALS

The advantages of your products and services generally need to be marketed to the CORs and program officials, rather than the contracting officials. The contracting officials are generally unfamiliar with the detailed use of the products and services you are selling or marketing. You can meet with them to build relationships, but generally they will not be the decision makers that initiate the acquisition process.

CORs and program officials are the government personnel that have the need for the product or service. They develop the statements of work and provide funding for the requirement. They also generate and process the paperwork for any new procurement. The contracting officials will purchase a product or service only after they receive the proper acquisition packages including a statement of work and schedule of deliverables from the user or program official. Therefore, the best way to have your product and service distinctions recognized is to meet with the program officials that will use your product or service.

If you market your product distinctions, you may have the ability to help the government officials fully understand

136

the current state of the marketplace. You can only do this if you gain access to the end users and program officials. For instance, in the information technology arena, the program official's expertise is their knowledge of hardware and software. End users and program officials should rely on industry representatives to help them leverage best practices. The FAR 15.201 encourages government officials to talk to industry officials. If you can gain access to program officials, you can hopefully establish a corporate product or service distinction.

CORs and program officials may call contractors to gather information when developing government cost estimates. Before they can process the paperwork for the contracting officials, they have to develop detailed cost estimates. Generally, they do not often have the full knowledge base required to develop the cost estimates. They sometimes turn to industry representatives for help with this step. Industry representatives know the cost and pricing guidelines as well as the performance advantages of its products and services. If you have price advantages that provide real value to the government, and if you can build a relationship to help the CORs and program officials understand how their requirements can be priced, you can create a company distinction. This interaction will help you to develop a relationship with federal officials.

BEWARE OF CONFLICTS OF INTEREST

I would like to provide you with a word of caution. Before you give any information to a federal contracting official, make sure that it is not creating an organizational conflict of interest, as described in the FAR subpart 9.5. If you work with federal officials in creating a government cost estimate or statement of work, you may be prohibited from bidding/proposing on the work. Therefore, be careful about what you give them and how the federal officials use the information. You may need to educate your sales staff about the FAR conflict of Interest provisions. Conflict of interest occurs when contractors have unfair access to nonpublic information, create biased ground rules by helping to write the government's statement of work, and when a contractor evaluates its own work creating impaired objectivity. Review the FAR subpart 9.5 for examples of these three types of conflicts of interest.

THINK OUTSIDE OF THE BOX

Think outside of the box during the marketing process. Company distinctions do not include accessing the government offices and marketing your products and services. You need to instead determine how your products or services can be leveraged to help federal programs become more efficient and effective. In particular, use one of the Golden Four strategies outlined in Chapter 12 to accomplish this. If you can help the government officials find efficiencies using your company's products and services, they will remember your company. Remember that you cannot directly solicit the government offices to sell your products and services. If you did, every type of marketer would be in the government offices every day, and nothing would get accomplished. Therefore, you need to have a plan to help the federal officials understand how your products and services can help them.

An email or brochure with your company's information, differentiators, and the points noted in the FAR 15.201 will not help you reach the government officials. In my federal career, I received dozens of emails every day from contractors selling their products and services with their products unique distinctions. I have also received hundreds of brochures in the mail. I did not open 99% of the emails and I placed the brochures in a pile by my desk. If government officials need to find a contractor for a particular requirement, particularly a small business set-aside, they either know the contractor from previous awards or do a Sources Sought Notice in FedBizOpps to locate additional contractors. The SBS may track and manage small businesses using emails and brochures, but usually remember the contractors as a result of face-to-face meetings. Do not expect snail mail or email to be your company's marketing tool of choice to showcase the advantages and distinctions.

Building and developing relationships with CORs, program and contracting officials is what you must do to become successful. Marketing your corporate advantages and distinctions is a key technique to help you gain access to the right government officials. If you can market your corporate advantages and distinctions with the right personnel, your chances of receiving a government contract or subcontract will increase substantially.

CHAPTER 15

GAIN ACCESS TO THE FEDERAL BUILDINGS

The attacks of 9/11 continue to impact each of us every day in a number of ways. For sales staff wanting to gain access to federal buildings, it has become much harder since 9/11. The years when contractors could walk in and meander through the government buildings and meet anyone who was willing to talk to them are long gone. This means that it is also harder to gain access to meet federal contracting and program officials. You need access to federal buildings to establish relationships with agency staff to get a leg up on your competition. One way to gain access to federal officials is to obtain an identification badge that will allow you walk unescorted in the federal buildings.

Throughout this chapter, I will use the word "access" to describe contractor employees that have obtained an identification badge that permits unescorted entry to government buildings. Agencies have different badging processes that give contractor personnel this kind of access. You need to learn what it takes to obtain a badge at your targeted agency.

HOW DO I OBTAIN AN ACCESS BADGE?

Gaining access to a federal building is both an art and a skill. Before you can begin to enter the federal buildings, determine what it takes to obtain an access badge at your targeted federal agency. Once you have determined what it takes to acquire an access badge, you have to determine if company employees can meet the agency's badging requirements. Talk to sales staff from other companies and

141

find out what it takes to gain an access badge at your targeted agency. You may receive a range of different answers from sales staff depending largely upon their experiences. You may also want to call the security office at the targeted agency. The security officers may not tell you how to gain an access badge, but it does not hurt to try. Evaluate the information you have received to determine what your targeted agency requires to secure a badge.

DO I NEED TO HAVE A CONTRACT?

It will be extremely tough, if not impossible, to acquire a badge if you do not already have a government contract or subcontract. Federal officials deem that you do not need a badge if you do not have a contract. If you have recently received a government contract, one of the first steps your staff should complete, is obtaining an identification badge so that they can easily enter the federal buildings. It will help with your performance on a contract because your staff can maintain contacts and relationships with their customer. Your staff will be able to communicate effectively with the government program personnel and meet with them regularly on a face-to-face basis. These business encounters will help your personnel establish the company with the agency and make the company more memorable to the government personnel. Once your program staff receive an access badge, it will be easier for them to establish relationships with all of the appropriate federal officials.

If your program personnel have a badge, they can usually get your sales staff into the federal building on an escort basis. However, this access will be on a limited basis. Once this happens, you should continue to send your sales staff to the program related technical meetings. Once the government personnel see that the sales staff is actively engaged on their contract, they may also decide to give the sales staff an access badge. This will lead to substantial opportunities to gather information and build relationships for the sales staff.

You need to actively engage the sales staff in the contract. You can do this by including them in the post-award meetings with the government officials. After all, it is their job to learn to expand the sales of your targeted federal agency and they cannot do this effectively unless they know how the agency operates. Sales staff can gather valuable information at post-award meetings. They can gather information including how the agency operates, who are the key players, and what new opportunities are on the horizon, etc. As soon as they become engaged on the contract, the federal officials may grant them an access badge.

WHAT DO I DO WHEN I RECEIVE A BADGE?

Based on my experience, only the smart sales staffs have received access badges since 9/11. The not-so-smart sales staffs have not received access badges. The companies whose sales staff had badges were often at my agency, in the cafeteria on their laptops, doing their work, or walking through the halls. Their job was to be at my agency managing contracts, while also building relationships and gathering information regarding future opportunities.

There was one particular company program manager who always knew of future opportunities on the horizon at my agency. This person had a dual role as a program manager and business developer for a big IT company. The company previously had a lot of major contracts at my agency. Over time, the company lost some of its major contracts, but this individual stayed onboard to manage the remaining smaller contracts. His company and the salesperson continued to target my agency. I often saw him inside of the building at my agency. After a few years, he resigned from the big IT company and went to work for a small start-up set-aside company that was a few years old. The new company was having a tough time accessing the federal marketplace.

As a result of his efforts over the course of one year, the small start-up set-aside company received a few new contract and subcontract awards at my agency. Within weeks of working for this new company, he had an access badge and was walking the halls of my agency. I knew what the process was to obtain an access badge and I would often review contractor badge requests on my assigned contracts. This particular salesperson knew the value of having an access badge, and had put it on his list of priorities early during his employment at the new company.

Needless to say, the sales of this small start-up set-aside company exploded in less than three years, and they became one of the top 20 small business federal contractors a few years ago. This was in large part because of his marketing ability and knowledge of his targeted agency. His ability to access the building was aided by his knack to build relationships, gather information, and convince government and contractor officials that they should contract with his company. If he did not have a badge, I am sure that his company's sales would not have increased at such a fast pace.

Once you have access to the building, you can build relationships with the government staff. Depending on the size of the agency that you are targeting, you may have the opportunity to meet with a lot of government personnel. Do not wear out your welcome. Government program and contracting personnel are extremely busy and there is a fine line between building relationships and becoming a nuisance. You need to have the right personnel in your company that know how to walk this fine line. If you or your staff becomes a nuisance, the government personnel will do what they can to avoid your company. Therefore, once a badge is obtained, build relationships slowly. Do not call the same person once a week expressing that you want to meet because you are in the building. Do not start wandering the halls just because you have a badge. Government contracting is not a sprint; it is a jog when it comes to building relationships. It is based on trust and built over time. Once you obtain a badge, think carefully how to use it so that you do not lose the government official's trust. If you lose the trust, it will be very difficult to regain it and develop successful relationships.

A program that I was supporting had a large preproposal conference. I was outside of the meeting location and a CEO of a Service-Disabled Veteran-Owned contractor introduced herself to me. She was attending the meeting even though she was not an interested bidder. I returned to my seat and within an hour and the CEO was missing from the meeting. She had received a visitors badge when she entered the building. I am pretty sure that she used the advantage of being in the building to wander the halls and talk face-to-face with her contacts. She knew that if she came to the conference, she would have the opportunity to walk the halls because she did not have a permanent badge to access the building. Although I do not condone her actions, she was thinking outside of the box. In regards to trust, if she was actually walking through the federal building halls unescorted, I would lose trust in her and her company. The agency procedures for entering the building and walking the halls have tightened since this conference.

Once you are in the building and starting to develop relationships, gather as much information as you can. Sales staff can become experts in all areas at your targeted agency by gathering information. If the sales staff are talented, they will soon know more about the agency's programs than most of the federal officials. The federal officials at the lower levels are generally concerned about their own contracts and programs, and they do not have the time or the detailed knowledge about programs and contracts in other areas of the agency.

HOW WILL THE ACCESS BADGE HELP MY COMPANY?

Gaining access to a government building will assist your sales team in gathering information. Your sales staff will learn how the agency operates and who are the key decision makers. They will also have direct access to information about new opportunities on the horizon. Every minute your sales staff are physically in a government building will provide an opportunity for your company. They will learn which government officials will and will not talk to them and they will learn about other opportunities in the agency. They will meet other contractors that you may not have previously known, some of whom may be your competitors. This will present an opportunity for partnering. Although some of the information you gather may be valuable and other information may not be valuable, it is all useful because you are increasing your knowledge about your targeted agency.

Most importantly, this access to the government building will lead to facial recognition with federal officials. I knew the sales staff that had access at my agency, even though I did not award or administer contracts with their companies. Their presence was better than the spam emails or sales brochures that I would receive from their companies and never open. I knew who they were and

146

what company they represented. In some cases, I knew them and they did not know me. If I had needed their products or services, I would have known where to turn.

I met with the program manager of a company that employed 20 personnel, had been an 8(a) certified contractor for two years, and had not yet received a government contract. The program manager and business development lead were quite astute in the art of government contracting. The program manager was a company partner who had an access badge, yet had not received a government contract over a two year period. He was on-site at the agency two to three days per week. However, at lunch, he left the facility and ate in local establishments. The agency had one cafeteria for all of the employees. He should have eaten in the cafeteria to build relationships with government employees. Building relationships represents a key component to marketing your company. You cannot build relationships if you leave the building during lunch. Lunch is a good time to get to know the government staff. The program manager had an access badge, but he was not using it to his advantage.

I knew a CEO whose company became an 8(a) certified contractor within two years of starting the business. The CEO knew the importance of obtaining a badge. Prior to the company becoming 8(a) certified by the SBA, he already had access to the federal building as a result of being a subcontractor on a government contract. Before he became an 8(a) contractor, many agency employees and other contractors knew him because he had a badge, an outgoing personality and most importantly performed on subcontracts in an exemplary manner. He had previously spent many days in the cafeteria meeting and talking to government staff. As a result, I am sure the company will have a successful future.

Another advantage of obtaining an access badge is that company personnel are able to resolve contracting and performance problems before they become major issues. I would often call the sales staff with access badges rather than the company's contracting staff if I had a contracting or performance problem. I did not know the contracting staff, but knew the sales staff. The contracting staff were usually located in another state and I generally had no contact with them. The on-site sales staff would either solve my problem quickly or work with their company personnel to resolve the issue. I find it more efficient to talk to on-site sales staff to resolve problems.

If you are a federal contractor, you may not want a performance issue documented by a long string of emails or letters that are sent to your contracting personnel. They can lead to misinterpretations, misunderstandings, and could impact your interim performance evaluation, final performance evaluation, and ability to receive future contracts. Some large contractors keep their sales staff at the agency a few days a week just to ensure that the federal officials are satisfied with their contract performance. If problems do occur, the sales staff quickly resolve them. This is another advantage of having personnel located in federal buildings.

I devoted this chapter to the topic of gaining access to federal buildings because the importance of this marketing technique is often overlooked by contractors. In my opinion, if you can gain access, it will create a competitive advantage over your competition regardless of whether you are a large or small business. This technique will help you to build relationships and gather information, which are the major keys to your success in federal contracting.

CHAPTER 16

CROSS TRAIN TECHNICAL STAFF

If your company currently has federal contracts or subcontracts, you may have employees physically located in federal buildings or they may have identification badges that provide access to federal buildings. More than likely the personnel who are physically located in federal buildings or have access badges are your technical staff. If you cannot obtain access badges for your sales staff, you may want to try some alternatives to help gather information and build relationships. If your technical staff is physically located on the government site or has access badges, one key alternative is providing cross training and place information gathering and building relationship goals in their performance plans.

Your sales staff are generally always under a close watch when they are in federal offices. It comes with the territory. If your technical staff has regular meetings with the federal staff, they are generally considered trusted partners. They often work side by side with the federal staff. This means that they have more on-site opportunities than the sales staff to make your company successful.

Your technical personnel that are physically located or have access into a federal building should already have knowledge and insight of the targeted agency. In addition, they should have developed business relationships with agency officials. If they do not, they have the opportunity to acquire knowledge, insight, and business relationships. However, these employees are not business development staff. Therefore, you need to make changes to their job

149

descriptions and performance plans to help your company be successful. This can be accomplished by placing sales and/or marketing goals in the technical staff's job descriptions and performance plans. You must also train them to meet the new performance goals. Very few federal contractors use this technique. However, every contractor that I have talked to about cross training the technical staff, including large and small contractors, agree that it is a good performance goal for the technical staff.

You need to adequately train your technical staff before they perform the limited role as a business developer. They may already have goods relationships with the government technical staff. If they do, that is a good start. You must set some expectations and possibly send them to training courses keyed around salesmanship. Their performance should be evaluated on a regular basis to determine if they are increasing the number of relationships at your targeted agency. They also need a performance goal for developing new leads. They must document what information they have learned and what is new at your targeted agency. In addition, they need to develop strategies to gather information. As a result of gathering information, they can also help write technical proposals at your targeted agency.

Many large companies have personnel that function in dual roles as sales staff and technical staff. Their dual roles should include, but not limited to the following activities: delivering the products and services; resolving problems; keeping the customer happy; and gathering information regarding new opportunities. In a previous chapter, I described a program manager of a large IT company who became employed at a smaller IT company. His company became one of the nation's top twenty small business contractors. He played the role of a program manager and capture manager. When he started his employment at the small contractor, his role was more of a capture manager rather than a program manager. Once the company started receiving contract and subcontract awards, his role changed to a program manager. His role could change from day-to-day and week-to-week, depending on the company's need at any point in time.

It is a prudent business decision to cross-train your project managers and other technical staff to function as sales staff regardless if you are a large or small business. Generally, technical and sales staff do not function as a team. Small companies need to be efficient and effective to remain competitive. Training your technical staff to understand the value of gathering information and developing relationships will contribute to your company's staff working together as a team. The appropriate technical staff at a government facility must therefore have performance plans that include suitable business development performance metrics.

PERFORMANCE ELEMENTS

The elements of the performance plan for the project manager and technical personnel must be simple, and should not be directly tied to a sales dollar goal. Sales dollar goals in the performance plans will not help you achieve your objectives. Keep the performance plan elements simple and provide the technical personnel with strategies to achieve the goals. Some elements in the performance plan should be directly tied to the themes of this book including gathering information, locating contacts, finding new opportunities, and establishing relationships.

The first element that I would recommend adding to the technical staff's performance plan is locating contacts. Your technical staff should know the targeted agency's organizational structure and the name of the key decision makers. Using this performance element will make them a more valuable employee and increase their understanding of their role in your company. Ask them to gather information including organization charts, telephone numbers, and names of key employees in your targeted agency. If you ask them to gather this information, you will be surprised what they already know or already have available at their fingertips.

Another element that should be included in their performance plan is to gather information regarding your contract, other contracts, and contractors working at your targeted agency. In other words, you will want to gather any other information that may give you a competitive edge. You should include the information that you want them to gather in their performance plan. Knowledge is power and the more knowledge you have gained the greater chance you have of meeting your sales goals at your targeted agency.

The most important performance plan element is finding new opportunities. Technical staff often discuss with federal officials the future needs of the agency. These discussions could result from new laws being passed by Congress, increased funding, new technology needs, or new directions of a federal agency. We could list thousands of reasons why there may be new opportunities at your targeted agency. Your technical staff is often aware of the changes that create opportunities for your company. However, they are not trained or do not often understand how their knowledge can help your company. If you teach the technical staff the value in finding new opportunities, your organization will be more successful. It is imperative that you rely on the existing technical staff to help your company achieve its sales goals. By placing this element in

152

their performance plan, you will be benefitting everyone in your company.

A final performance plan element for your program staff should be establishing relationships and building trust. If you adequately train staff to become trusted partners with the federal officials, it will go a long way to helping your company be successful. It always helps to keep the communication lines flowing between federal and contractor staff. If your technical staff can establish business relationships and build trust, your information gathering and knowledge of your targeted agency will be greatly enhanced.

The performance goals must be realistic. The performance goals can vary depending on many factors including the size of the agency, the role of the technical and project personnel on your contract, and the physical location of your staff in a federal building. The performance factors can vary, but they must be realistic so that your personnel have the opportunity to be successful.

Do not include these performance elements in every technical employee's performance plan. Some technical employees cannot be trusted to gather the information described in this chapter. Some of your technical and project personnel do not have the people skills to meet these performance plan elements. If you do not think that your technical employees have the appropriate skill sets or can learn them, do not include these elements in their performance plan. They can hurt your company rather than help your company. Use good judgment before you begin to change your company's performance plans. If you do not use good judgment, federal staff may learn not to trust your company and could become suspicious of your employees intentions. You do not want to endanger your company's reputation because of the elements that were included in the technical employee's performance plan. It goes without saying that you must not authorize or allow the technical and project personnel to do anything illegal or unethical to meet their performance plan objectives.

Before you place the elements in your technical or project staff's performance plan, you must give them adequate training. This training could be in the form of federal sales training, interpersonal relationship training, ethics training, or government contracting 101. You need to provide adequate training to your employees to be successful. Once the training is complete, add the appropriate elements to their performance plan.

Placing business development and capture management performance elements in your technical staff's performance plans will help your company achieve its sales objectives. I would recommend that you consider using finding contacts, gathering information, and finding new opportunities in the performance plans. However, you can also be creative and develop other performance elements that you think are realistic for the given situation. Placing the appropriate performance elements in your technical staff's performance plans will help your company become more efficient and effective in its business development and capture activities.

CHAPTER 17

THE ADVANTAGES OF THE JOBS ACT OF 2010

THE JOBS ACT OF 2010

On September 27, 2010, President Obama signed into law the Jumpstart Our Business Startups Act (JOBS Act). This law, which is available on the internet, was the most significant piece of small business legislation in over a decade and it may impact how you conduct business with the federal government. The primary purpose of the legislation was to help small businesses during the recent economic recovery by creating jobs, offering billions of dollars in lending support, and providing tax cuts.

The biggest impact that business development and capture sales staff need to know regarding this law is that it gives "parity" among federal small-business contracting programs. As a result of the JOBS Act, the federal government will no longer give preference to any one type of Small Disadvantaged Business (SDB) Concern when awarding federal contracts. This means that federal officials are now free to choose among businesses including Small Disadvantage Women-Owned companies, Women-Owned companies, Service-Disabled Veteran-Owned companies, HUBZone companies, and 8(a) companies when deciding an acquisition strategy for SDB Concern Set-Aside procurements. Before the law was passed, Small Disadvantage Women-Owned companies, Women-Owned Businesses, and Service-Disabled Veteran-Owned Businesses were not able to actively participate in the Small Business Set-Aside Programs. The Act eliminates any priority, so that each type of SDB Concern has an

155

equal opportunity to gain a federal contract award. The JOBS Act has created a major change in conducting business with the federal government.

CHANGES IN AUTHORITY

Prior to this law, the SBS essentially made all of the decisions about placing a solicitation in a particular SDB Concern Set-Aside Program. For instance, if a SBS decided to place a new requirement in the 8(a) program, only certified 8(a) organizations had the opportunity to compete for the contract. The SBS decided if an acquisition would be placed in the 8(a), HUBZone, Services-Disabled Veteran-Owned Business, Small Disadvantaged Women-Owned Business, or Women-Owned Business. They also recognized the need to award contracts in an efficient manner which resulted in most contracts being placed in the 8(a) Program. The SBS had a lot of power and authority in helping organizations win a federal contract. If the SBS did not like you or your company, that could lead to you missing contracting opportunities.

The JOBS Act legislation was a major change for SBSs and federal contracting officers. The JOBS Act still gives the SBS the authority to recommend to the contracting officer that a requirement be placed in the SDB Concern Program. Contracting officials almost always follow their recommendation. However, the JOBS Act removed the SBS's authority to place a requirement in a particular type of SDB Concern Program. As a result of the JOBS Act, once the SBS recommends that a new requirement be placed in the SDB Concern Program, the contracting officer now has the flexibility to place it in any specific set-aside program including the Service-Disabled Veteran-Owned, 8(a), Women-Owned, or HUBZone Programs. There is no particular priority order for contracting officers. Contracting officers now have the free will to choose the

Small Business Set-Aside Program that will best fulfill the needs of their agency including helping to meet their small business goals.

THE JOBS ACT CHANGES YOUR INTERACTION WITH GOVERNMENT OFFICIALS

The new law impacts many personnel involved in the acquisition cycle. Particularly, the JOBS Act creates a major a shift in the role of the contracting officer and your sales staff. It changes the process for how SDB Concerns are selected and how products and services can be procured from Women-Owned businesses and Service-Disabled Veteran-Owned Businesses. The JOBS Act provides contracting officers a lot of new opportunities to find qualified vendors (Women-Owned Businesses and Service-Disabled Veteran-Owned Businesses) to perform the agency's work. It provides your sales staff a bigger role in influencing the acquisition process. These changes impact the acquisition process in significant ways.

Contracting officers now have a larger role in helping any category of small business set-aside companies win a federal contract. Since the contracting officers are now the official that determines which SDB Concern Set-Aside Program an acquisition is placed in, it is your sales staff's job to help influence this decision. Prior to the JOBS Act, the SBS made the decision. Most contracting officials and probably all program officials do not know how the JOBS Act impacted their responsibilities.

The JOBS Act presents an opportunity for your company to have a role in the influencing which SDB Concern Program a solicitation is placed in. To influence the decision, your sales staff must meet with program and contracting officials and educate them regarding this aspect of the JOBS Act. If you are a Women-Owned Business, the contracting officers can now make the

157

decision to compete among other Women-Owned businesses. Contracting officers now have a larger role in helping any type of SDB Concern compete and win a federal contract award.

As a result of the JOBS Act, contracting officers have a larger role in helping each agency meet its small business goals. Federal agencies have small business goals for each Set-Aside Program as well as an overall small business goal for the agency. Contracting officers can now directly impact an agency's ability to achieve its small business goals. To successfully achieve these goals, an agency monitors the contract dollars awarded to small businesses throughout the fiscal year. If the agency is not meeting its goal for a specific Set-Aside Program, for instance HUBZones, the agency's contracting officers may take extra steps to locate HUBZone companies for solicitations. Senior agency officials have small business goals in their performance plans and depend on the contracting officers to help them meet the goals each fiscal year. Contracting officers now have a direct impact in helping the agency meet its small business goals.

If your company is certified as a Women-Owned or Service-Disabled Veteran-Owned organization, you now have a stronger competitive edge in the marketplace. Women-Owned organizations now have the same opportunity to win federal set-aside awards as 8(a) organizations have had in the past. Any company SDB Concern can now compete in the federal marketplace equally. However, if your company is in the HUBZone or 8(a) Program, you now have more competition from the other set-aside organizations.

Regardless of the category of your set-aside, the fact remains the same that the rules of the game have changed and are now more complex. Prior to the passing of the

JOBS Act, the SBS was the federal official at each agency that had the biggest impact in determining if particular requirements would be set-aside. They were also responsible for placing new requirements in a particular Set-Aside Program. You could establish a relationship with the SBS at each federal agency in hopes that they would select your company's SDB Concern Set-Aside category for a procurement. You can still do that, but the authority to make these determinations now rests with the contracting officer. To be totally effective, you must work with as many of the contracting officers at your targeted agency to make an impact. Your best approach is still to work with the targeted agency's SBS, who generally knows the planned acquisitions in a fiscal year and the federal contracting officers at the agency.

The best way for you to take advantage of the JOBS Act is to build relationships with federal contracting and program officials. You must reach out to contracting officials so that they can learn about your business's capabilities. Many small business contractors with active contracts at federal agencies do not like talking to the contracting officers. They think that it may create problems and that the old theory of "out of sight, out of mind" holds true. In general, contractor staff is more engaged with the government's program staff as opposed to the contracting staff. However, the JOBS Act changed the initial phase of the acquisition process to a large extent. You should now get engaged with contracting officers, particularly if you have an active contract with the government.

Get ahead of the curve and do what few others are doing at your targeted agency. Start building relationships with the contracting staff. If and when you do engage the contracting officers, put the right person on the job. Use a people person for this position, and make sure that he or she knows when to back off, is never offensive, and is friendly. You want to build the relationship without becoming a nuisance. It is a tough balance, and you need the right person with the right skill set to make your company successful. The JOBS Act creates the need for sales staff to get engaged with your contracting and programming staff early in the acquisition cycle to stay ahead of the competition.

CHAPTER 18

TIMING IS EVERYTHING

THE BUDGET CYCLE

The old saying tells us that "timing is everything," and the same is true when it comes to government contracting. It often comes down to submitting a proposal at the right time, on the right effort, or being in the government offices on the right day when the government needs to procure products or services provided by your company. "Timing is everything" would lead you to believe that it takes a lot of luck to achieve your goal. However, when it comes to federal contracting, your timing should be planned to help increase your chances of winning a government contract.

The first major timing issue is to learn how the federal acquisition cycle works at your targeted agency. Every government agency's fiscal year runs from October 1st to September 30th. The real question is how good is your targeted agency at planning the fiscal year's procurements prior to the October 1st start date. If they are really good at planning, they will have the fiscal year's acquisitions on a detailed plan before or shortly after October 1st. However, this is highly unlikely. Most agencies do not do a good job of planning for the year's acquisitions before a fiscal year starts or early in the current fiscal year. Congress has created this problem. Congress does not generally approve the President's budget until the February time frame or as in the recent past, does not approve it at all, which creates a significant problem with the acquisition cycle at each agency.

161

The first problem with this delay is that it stalls the acquisition process for most new actions. Agencies gather spending plans and begin to process recurring contract actions, but generally do not begin to prepare the solicitation documents for new actions until the fiscal year's budget is approved. Individual offices often do not spend time developing the acquisition strategies and statements of work until Congress approves the budget or the agency receives its spending plan for the entire fiscal year. As a result, very few solicitation packages are processed on new actions for the first few months of the fiscal year. Most of the agency acquisition documents are generally not developed during this period of time.

Congress and the President usually approve the federal budget in the February timeframe. Once the budget is approved, the government acquisition cycle cranks up into action for new planned acquisitions. By this time, it is late February and the federal agencies must rush to develop the final spending plans, develop acquisition strategies, and prepare the acquisition documents, including the statements of work. Agencies develop a lot of the acquisition documents for new actions in the February to May timeframe. Once these documents are prepared, it is often late May or June, and only three months are left in that fiscal year's acquisition cycle.

The months of late June through September are very, very busy for the agency's acquisition officials. They are preparing solicitations, reviewing proposals, negotiating with contractors, and preparing the award documents at this time. If August has come and gone, and you have not yet submitted one proposal, or are not negotiating with government officials, you have a very limited chance of receiving a government contract prior to the end of the fiscal year. Time is running out in August and September for federal acquisition officials to go through all of the acquisition steps necessary to award a contract by September 30th.

HUNT DURING THE RIGHT TIME OF YEAR

It is highly unlikely that you will have to submit proposals or will receive contract awards in the October 1st through December 31st timeframe. Agencies do not know their budget during these months and generally only obligate funding to keep the doors open. Agencies do not normally award new contracts during this time period because they are waiting for their fiscal year budgets to be approved by Congress and the President. As a result, do not put a lot of your company's energy, time, and resources expecting to prepare proposals and receive contracts during the October through December time period.

During the October through December time period, you should be gathering information. Just be forewarned that the information gathered during this time period is not always accurate because the federal officials do not know how much money they will receive until the Congress and President approve the federal budget. However, information is still worth gathering to ascertain where you may fit into the agency's potential acquisition plans. Federal acquisition officials may be more willing to talk to you during this time of year because they are not as busy. Large dollar full and open competition solicitations are being prepared during this timeframe. You will not be able to influence the acquisition strategy of these procurements. However, continue to gather information and build relationships, but understand the possible drawbacks during this time period.

As January and February draw near, start gearing up to learn as much as you can about new acquisitions on the horizon. You should have your plan in place to gather information and meet agency representatives beginning in February. By the time March approaches, your sales plan should be ramped up at your targeted agency. February through June is the critical timeframe, and your actions during these months will determine if you are going to win an agency contract. Particularly, if you are designated in a Set-Aside Program category, implement your plan of action during this time period. You can influence the acquisition process during this time of year.

The information gathering and relationship building you have previously established will begin to pay off as you deliver sales presentations and seek face time with agency officials. Take steps to ensure that you have opportunities to meet with agency staff during this time period. The meetings will keep your company fresh in their minds. Regardless of whether you are a large or small business on the GSA Schedule or have been awarded GWACs, agency acquisition officials who like your company can often find a way to include it in the acquisition process at this time. If your sales skills are not applied to the maximum extent practical during this time period, your chances of success will drastically diminish.

In the months of late June through September, you should be submitting proposals and negotiating with the agency officials. This will be the ultimate payoff to the earlier groundwork, information gathering, and relationship building that you completed.

FEDBIZOPPS NOTICES

There are no specific timing benefits when it comes to reviewing the FedBizOpps notices. When an agency posts them, they are available for your review. However, if you are gathering information at your targeted agency in the proper manner, you will know about the agency's upcoming solicitations before they are posted in the FedBizOpps. Therefore, if the FedBizOpps posting is your first notification about the agency's requirement, it may be too late to prepare a great proposal. Your ability to gather information is critical to your teaming and subcontracting arrangements for solicitations posted in the FedBizOpps. Your teaming and subcontracting arrangements must be developed before a solicitation is posted in the FedBizOpps. Information gathering will help you stay one step ahead of your competition.

PICK THE RIGHT ACQUISITIONS

Another timing issue is proposing on the right acquisition(s). You do not want to put all of your effort into one or two actions unless you have a reasonable chance to win the contract award. In government contracting, there are no guarantees, so you have to assess the risk of winning each solicitation. There are many books, training courses, and consultants that can help educate you about the probabilities of winning particular solicitations. You do not want to wear your staff out submitting proposals on solicitations in which you have a remote chance of winning. In addition, you do not want to have your staff preparing proposals on high-risk solicitations, only to see another solicitation issued in which you have a greater chance of winning. The more information you have gathered throughout the fiscal year, the better chance you have of submitting proposals for the solicitations in which you have adequately prepared to win.

CONTRACTOR QUARTERLY/YEAR ENDS

Sales staff can be a real nuisance to the government staff. Software and hardware sales staff is particularly nasty when their quarterly or yearly sales periods are ending. As a government official, I did not appreciate contractor sales staff giving discount offers a week prior to the end of their company's fiscal year. They would tell me that if the government bought their product today, on the last day of the company's fiscal year, it would be 20% cheaper than it will be the following week. It was obvious that the company was trying to beat its quarterly estimates for Wall Street or the sales staff was just trying to make their sales quota. I was always sympathetic to their need, but having the price of a commercial product vary by 20% from one day to the next appeared immoral.

Corporate officials and sales staff should know that government officials often do not appreciate these sales tactics. It cheapens the value of the company and its relationship with its customers, which their sales staff took a long time and a lot of effort to develop. The timing on the part of the commercial sales staff may be a part of the selling process, but it is not a good way to do business with federal contracting officials. The federal contracting officials are smarter than you think and for years will not forget the sales tactic a company used at the end of a particular quarter or fiscal year.

SEPTEMBER IS A RUSH

There is one final issue regarding the timing of the government fiscal year's acquisition cycle. As September nears, leave the federal contracting officials alone. They are under enormous pressure to obligate the funding in their agency's budget. If you contact them frequently at this time of the fiscal year, you may ruin your relationship with them. There are a few tools that they have in their acquisition tool chest to start and finish an acquisition in September. However, that generally will not help you because few acquisitions start and end in September. If you have not done your homework in the first eleven months of the fiscal year, do not start in September. Leave the contracting officials alone in September and let them call you. Do not call them unless it is an emergency situation.

When it comes to government contracting, timing is everything. Think about the fiscal year cycle when you develop your market and sales plan. If you manage your meeting times properly during the fiscal year, it should help you to increase your chances of winning a government contract.

CHAPTER 19

FIND OTHER SOURCES OF INFORMATION

HIRE A COMPANY TO DO THE RESEARCH

There are a lot of other ways to gather information regarding your targeted agency. One option is to pay a company that specializes in gathering information of federal agencies and have them do your research for you. This type of company gathers a range of information from various sources regarding your targeted agency. They work at the federal, state, and local agency levels to gather information and sell it to independent contractors. The information that they can provide includes general overviews of federal agencies, targeted information about specific agencies, and spending trends at those agencies. They may even help you to find teaming partners.

Up to a few years ago, there were three primary research sources in the federal marketplace including GovWin, which is owned by Deltek, Input, and FedSources. Input was bought by Deltek in 2010 and FedSources was bought by Deltek in 2011. DelTek eliminated the competition. That did not leave a lot of options for federal contractors. However, a new contractor, Bloomberg Government has emerged. There are now two primary companies, Deltek and Bloomberg Government that will provide you with information regarding your targeted agency. In addition, a capture consultant told me she uses a product called "e-pipeline." However, I am unfamiliar with e-pipeline or its federal contracting market share. Deltek's GovWin is the most popular product, while Bloomberg Government is an up and coming product in the marketplace.

Each of these companies has thousands of paying clients. They track thousands of federal, state, and local government acquisitions. If you sign a contract with them, they will target and organize the information from FedBizOpps, FPDS, and Freedom of Information Act requests. GovWin will also call contracting officials at your targeted agencies and ask them for specific information. GovWin has a large database of information. They develop information regarding specific acquisitions one to two years before they are recompeted or renewed. This means that their clients have knowledge about the acquisition years before their competition, and as a result a competitive edge.

How does GovWin do this? They get copies of contracts using Freedom of Information Act requests. If they find contracts that will expire soon, they begin calling the federal officials noted in the contracts and gather information about those contracts. If you are gathering information effectively at your targeted agency, you should know more than GovWin.

GovWin and Bloomberg Government also have their own database comprised of the information contained in the FPDS. I have seen a demonstration of the Bloomberg Government product. It provides easy access to information contained in the FPDS fields. It can instantaneously show you how many contracts were awarded at your targeted agency with only one proposal received. It can show you instantaneously how many contracts were awarded at an agency using a particular NAICS code. Any information put into the FPDS database can be easily sorted in Bloomberg Government's database. I would recommend you go to these contractors' websites to determine how their tools will help you to gather information at your targeted agency. If you do not have time, resources, or knowledge to gather the information yourself, companies like Deltek's GovWin and Bloomberg Government can help by doing the work for you.

AGENCY ACQUISITION PLANS

Agencies have yearly acquisition plans, which lists the acquisitions planned for a given fiscal year. These are active documents and change constantly during the course of the fiscal year. They list the year's planned acquisition actions, anticipated acquisition schedules, contract types, and proposed award dates to name a few. It is up to the contracting and program officials to keep this document up to date, and ensure that the agency acquisitions are completed prior to the end of each fiscal year. Agency SBSs also use an agency's acquisition plan to notify industry representatives about upcoming procurements. Agency SBSs may use the information on the acquisition plan to post it to an agency's website. A contracting official may share some of this information with you if an opportunity exists with your company during the fiscal year. The FAR Subpart 5.4 "Release of Information" clause addresses some of these issues and states that:

Contracting Officers may make available maximum information to the public, except information – (1) On plans that would provide undue or discriminatory information to private or personal interests.

This means that contracting officials have to be very careful about the type of information they release. However, the federal officials are generally very organized and know how many acquisitions they must execute. They can look at their acquisition plans and let you know in general if there are opportunities for you in a fiscal year. If you are an 8(a) certified small business and they have a requirement on their acquisition plan that is under the 8(a) competitive thresholds, they could almost immediately

171

decide to award the contract to your business noncompetitively. You can ask a federal official if he or she has any 8(a) Set-Aside requirements that are less than $4,000,000. I have seen very few sales staff ask this question. However, if you are an 8(a) or have contracting instrument in place that authorizes contracting officers to generate noncompetitive awards, you should consider asking the question directly, since that is really what you want and need know.

If you do your homework and gather information prior to meeting with a contracting official, you can even discuss the acquisition strategies of particular procurements as is noted in the FAR 15.201. Discussing acquisition strategies can provide you with a lot of information about future procurements. If you have done your homework, contracting officials can tell you, "There will be an opportunity this fiscal year in that area," or "Keep your eyes open in FedBizOpps," or "We're doing this procurement on an existing IDIQ." Any advance information will help you to adequately evaluate future opportunities.

Acquisition plans kept at the agency provide valuable information to contracting officials. It is important for you to know that they exist and are managed on a daily basis by the contracting staff. If you are able to engage the agency contracting officials regarding actions on their contracting plan, it will give you a competitive edge.

ATTEND INDUSTRY CONFERENCES

There is a wide variety of industry sponsored conferences available to help you to gain knowledge, gather information, and build relationships. One of the first questions you need to ask yourself is whether you should attend a particular conference. If you are going to attend conferences, make sure they are appropriate for you and your company. In addition, you need to decide if you should go as an attendee or have a sales booth. You will find that some contractor conferences offer the best advantages to attendees, while others offer better advantages for contractors maintaining a booth. Some conferences are not worth attending or purchasing a booth, and therefore should not be an option. If you have any questions about the value of having a sales booth at a conference, start by attending the conference as a guest. If you find that the conference is valuable, obtain a sales booth for your company the following year. Do not waste your time and resources attending conferences that provide little value in your specific niche.

Before you attend a conference, uncover a couple of facts including:

- Who attends the conference, government or industry?

- How many people attend the conference?

- How long has the conference been in existence?

- How much will it cost to attend?

- How much will it cost for a sales booth?

- How will the stated purpose of the conference help your company succeed?

- What knowledge will you gain at the conference?

- Can you be a speaker at the conference?

- Will your targeted agency personnel be in attendance at the conference?

- Can you gather valuable information at the conference?

- Can you build relationships at the conference?

173

Once you have answered these questions, you will have a better idea of whether you should attend the conference. You should also keep in mind that you need to focus on your targeted agency. If your targeted agency is not attending or represented at an event, think twice before attending.

In terms of advice on which conference to attend, use the bullets above to make that determination. When I talk to contractors, I have consistently been told that the Armed Forces Communications and Electronics Association (AFCEA) have great conferences that help contractors gain knowledge and gather information about federal agencies. Their website is www.afcea.org. I have heard this from novice and experienced business development staff. Before you attend an AFCEA conference, make sure that the subject matter benefits your company.

There are a lot of other good conferences. In the field of healthcare, the yearly Healthcare Information and Management Systems Society (HIMSS) conference attracts twenty-five thousand people each year. Their website is www.himssconference.org. If you are employed in any healthcare-related field, this is a must-attend conference. The HIMSS conference also has federal healthcare business development training sessions for your sales staff.

The Federal Business Council, Inc. (FBC)) is another organization that regularly conducts conferences. Their website, www.fbcinc.com, states the "Federal Business Council, Inc. (FBC) specializes in producing conferences and trade show events at and for federal government locations throughout the United States. Each month thousands of federal employees attend FBC events to evaluate the latest advances in technology, military hardware, training, and other product areas, as well as update their sources for future requirements. Founded in 1976, FBC has conducted more than 4,000 onsite expositions and conferences for the Department of Defense, Intelligence, and civilian agencies." Review their website and consider attending their appropriate conferences.

Another great way to locate appropriate government conferences is through the GovEvents website, GovEvents.com. The GovEvents website allows you to "Search, track and register for events of interest to you! Find the latest government conferences, tradeshows, webcasts and more..." I have seen their trade booth at many government conferences. GovEvents is a great source to locate suitable government conferences to attend.

When attending one of the major conferences, your name will be placed on a mailing list, and you will receive advance communications about additional federal contracting conferences. Do your homework, attend some of the bigger conferences and find out from other attendees which conferences you should consider attending in the future.

There are a lot of conferences sponsored by federal agencies and commercial organizations. There are so many conferences taking place throughout the year that you have to be selective deciding which conferences to attend. Attending the wrong conference is a waste of time and money for your company. Attending the right conference should provide valuable insight to help you to gain knowledge, gather information, and build relationships.

SOCIAL MEDIA

Federal contracting officials are now exploring how to officially use social media outlets such as Facebook, MeetUp, and LinkedIn. You may find these officials on some social marketing websites if they are authorized for use by their agency's ethics officials. Federal contracting officers are generally leery to join these sites due to a lack of clear guidance regarding "outside activities." This will change over time. If you want to stay ahead of the competition, determine how you can engage federal contracting officials on an ethical basis using social media outlets as they become available for use to federal officials.

THINK OUTSIDE OF THE BOX

Think outside of the box when searching for other sources of information. An acquaintance of mine sells computer hardware and software to the federal government. He told me that he was travelling to a Mid-West location to meet a senior acquisition official. He said that this senior official goes to a particular bar every Tuesday afternoon to meet contractor personnel and discuss business. My friend was flying across the country to meet this senior agency official at a bar. I think that is a very creative way to meet federal officials and may pay dividends. In summary, you need to gather information and build relationships in any way possible. Brainstorm with your staff and develop creative ways to enhance your information gathering and relationship building techniques.

JOIN A PROFESSIONAL ORGANIZATION

Another strategy is to locate professional organizations and look specifically for a group that specializes in federal contracting. The National Contract Management Association (NCMA) is one such organization. This association is comprised of 25,000 government and private contracting professionals, with the primary role of advancing the education and professionalism in the acquisition field. The NCMA will help you to keep up with the changes in the federal contracting field, and will also help to enhance your existing acquisition skills. In addition, the local NCMA chapter members are comprised of both federal officials and contractor personnel. Senior-level federal officials often attend meetings as guest speakers. The NCMA government members are usually comprised of contracting officers and contract specialists. You will get to know some federal contracting officers by joining the organization, and you will also be able to increase your knowledge about your profession.

My local NCMA Woodlawn Chapter rotates between a Lunch & Learn event and networking event over a two month period. I have known contractors that fly in from other states just to attend the NCMA events. The contractors fly to the two hour event because they know it is the one opportunity they will have to regularly meet contractors and government officials that do business at their targeted agency. This professional organization chapter has really helped contractors meet and learn about each other's capabilities and about their targeted agency.

A close friend of mine recently told me that his sales goal/"book of business" goal was going to increase substantially. He is in his late fifties. He told me that the company had hired a younger twenty-something year old person to work his same territory. That new person was on Facebook, LinkedIn, and some other websites. He had hundreds of contacts, but had not yet booked any business during the year. This new salesperson may do well over time, but in the short run, he needs to build relationships to be successful. New social media techniques cannot replace personal face-to-face contacts. The same is true with government contracting. You need to build relationships with government staff to increase your chances of being successful. This is particularly true for small business contractors.

There are other advantages to joining these organizations as compared to joining LinkedIn and Facebook. With an organization like NCMA, you have face-to-face contact with other contracting professionals. This will help you establish real relationships, built around understanding and trust, which is better than what LinkedIn and Facebook have to offer.

FEDERAL NEWS RADIO

Even though I live and commute in the Baltimore area, during my commute I often listen to a Washington D.C. radio station, Federal News Radio, 1500 a.m. The radio show is devoted to providing information about the federal marketplace to federal employees and federal contractors. The radio show has announcers whose expertise is specifically geared to federal acquisition, federal technology, Congress, and individual federal agencies. The announcers cover a broad variety of topics. It does not matter where you live because the information from the show is available on the internet at federal newsRadio.com. The radio station provides insight regarding new acquisition trends, insight of acquisition rules and regulations, and changes taking place in federal agencies. Reviewing this website regarding your targeted agency may provide you with valuable information.

The sources shown above are just a few sources that can help you to gain knowledge, gather information and build relationships. However, these are not the only sources that you should be using to find information. Use sources of information that other contractors are using and develop best practices for your organization. If you are fortunate, you may find information sources that are unknown or unavailable to most contractors.

NEW COMMUNICATION STRATEGIES

In the past, government agencies have not shared their information effectively. In 2011, information sharing among industry representatives and federal agencies started to change. The Office of Federal Procurement Policy has made a push in this direction, and now encourages agencies to share their yearly acquisition information with industry representatives. As a result of the leadership's efforts to drive transparency, agency information should become more readily available in the upcoming years. Keep an eye on your targeted agency's website, as it will begin to provide more information about their acquisitions in the future.

In the future, agencies should also begin increasing the number of useful industry meetings, conferences, and other outreach activities that provide an easy opportunity to discuss acquisition opportunities in each fiscal year. The new buzz word is "innovation" and the leadership of agencies is looking for new ways to reach industry through innovation. The information age is going to continue to change the methods used by agencies to conduct business, and it is your job to keep up with these new methods of communication. Watch how your targeted agency responds to these new changes, and adjust your own information gathering techniques. If you can stay on top of the wave of new information, it may result in your company winning a federal contract.

CHAPTER 20

PARTNER WITH OTHER CONTRACTORS

Now that you have read this much of the book, you probably realize that government contracting is a tough business. You need to do whatever you can to keep your employees working and provide a continuous cash flow for your company if you are going to be successful. One way to keep your employees working and increase your cash flow is to use the business relationships that you have established to leverage subcontracting and teaming opportunities. Subcontracting opportunities can be leveraged regardless of whether you are currently a prime contractor or a subcontractor. Teaming opportunities can be leveraged with companies larger or smaller than your company. As you learn about your targeted agency and your relationships grow, other contractors will learn about your company's abilities. You will also learn about their capabilities and the key contractors to decide whether you can work with them.

Subcontracting is more important today than it has ever been in the federal marketplace. Agencies are now using a lot of contracting vehicles that do not require the agency to post solicitations on FedBizOpps. These are typically GWAC or agency IDIQ contracting arrangements. The GWACs include the GSA Schedules. These contracting arrangements lock you out of doing business at your targeted agency unless you are a prime contractor on the particular contracting vehicle the agency uses. Therefore, if you do not have an IDIQ contract or the particular GWAC that the agency uses, your only possibility of receiving work is to partner with a prime contractor. As the

181

government continues to streamline and look for ways to consolidate various contracting arrangements, subcontracting arrangements will become a more important priority for government contractors.

ADVANTAGES OF BEING A SUBCONTRACTOR TO A PRIME CONTRACTOR

Subcontracting can take place in two forms. The first form is being a subcontractor to a contractor who has an active contract or is going to submit a proposal resulting from a solicitation being issued by the government. If you are a new federal contractor, being a subcontractor will help you build a performance history, which is vital if you want to respond to solicitations as a prime contractor. Receiving subcontracts will also allow you to spread your overhead across more contracts, thereby reducing your indirect rates, which is vitally important in a competitive marketplace. There are also fewer government administrative burdens placed on subcontractors. Being a subcontractor provides a lot of information that you might not have otherwise known and allows contractors to enhance company skills sets at your targeted agency.

Being a subcontractor also has a few disadvantages. As a subcontractor, you often have no control of the price or cost proposal submitted by the prime contractor. You also have no control of how thoroughly they have prepared the technical proposal submission. You usually do not have input in the negotiation process either. The biggest disadvantage that I consistently see and hear is from subcontractors who were included in the prime contractor's initial proposal, but once an award is made they never receive an actual subcontract. That is the major disadvantage of being a proposed subcontractor.

If you are negotiating to become a subcontractor, be careful about how you negotiate your subcontract, as it

182

must protect your company and the prime contractor. Design a fixed-price contract if you are a new contractor because your accounting system will probably be inadequate to receive cost reimbursement type contracts. If you do not have an accounting system that the government has determined to be adequate, you may be required to have an adequate accounting system before proposing as a subcontractor on cost-reimbursement or time and material subcontracts.

I have seen a lot of good and bad practices when it comes to subcontracting. The best practices involved companies that have developed relationships with other contractors, have some solid subcontracts in place, have a significant number of employees, and understand how to market and sell to the government prior to becoming an 8(a) certified contractor. They take their time and learn the federal marketplace before they go to the SBA to receive an 8(a) certification. They understand and use the 8(a) certification when they are ready to take the organization to the next level. However, they start by building relationships and receiving subcontracts prior to wasting the time permitted to them under the 8(a) program.

One of the worst practices involved contractors that received their 8(a) certification prior to receiving several subcontracts and prior to really understanding the federal marketplace or how to market and sell to the government. They end up wasting the time allotted for the organization to be a SBA certified 8(a) contractor. As a result of their missteps, their 8(a) business does not expand and grow as one would expect under this program that gives contractors a significant advantage in the federal marketplace.

ADVANTAGES OF BEING A PRIME CONTRACTOR WITH SUBCONTRACTORS

The second form of subcontracting is when a prime contractor subcontracts a portion of the contract or solicitation to another contractor. If you are the prime contractor, you can benefit from subcontracting a portion of your work to other contractors. If your company does not have all of the skill sets necessary to propose on a solicitation, you may want to consider subcontracting that portion of the work. It eliminates the need to hire employees to perform sections of a statement of work that are not your company's area of expertise. It also allows you to concentrate on what your company is good at doing rather than expending time and resources learning new skill sets. If you subcontract with other vendors, it will also help you to build long-term relationships. These relationships will help you to gather information regarding future requirements and solicitations. Your established relationships may help you to secure future contracts or subcontracts based on your subcontractor's knowledge and/or skill sets. However, being a prime contractor is almost always better than being a subcontractor because it provides control to the prime contractor of its success.

SUBCONTRACTING GOALS

Large business government prime contractors must also meet small business subcontracting goals, which are similar to the overall small business goals of a federal agency. Therefore, if you are a small business, you have a tremendous advantage in the federal marketplace when you are a subcontractor. Government contractors need your assistance to meet their small business subcontracting goals. The subcontracting goals are cited in their government contracts. This creates leverage for you in the competitive federal marketplace. If your company is certified in a small business set-aside category and has developed relationships with prime contractors, you have a competitive advantage in the federal marketplace by helping the prime contractors meet their small business set-aside goals.

The federal government is now enforcing prime contractor's achievement of small business subcontracting goals through an Electronic Subcontracting Reporting System (eSRS). The eSRS is a web-based system that allows federal government prime contractors to report subcontracting actions on federal government contracts. This provides the federal government with knowledge of how a contractor's subcontracting dollars are being distributed among small and small disadvantaged businesses in relation to the subcontracting goals. The federal contracting officials and agency SBSs compare the subcontracting goals proposed at the time of award with the subcontracting efforts realized during the contract performance periods. Monitoring prime contractor's subcontracting performance keeps the prime contractors committed to their goals. If the contractor is not meeting its subcontracting goals, federal officials will meet with the contractor to determine why they are missing their subcontracting goals. If the goals are not achieved, the contractor may be negatively impacted, including having their option year not exercised and/or a negative past performance rating.

The eSRS also automates the collection of prime contractor subcontract reporting data, which was previously collected only in hard copy. As a result, there is more visibility and accountability imposed on every contractor in regards to achieving their subcontracting goals. In the past, prime contractors could propose subcontractor goals and then forget about them. There was no consequence for failing to meet those goals. The increased oversight will result in prime contractors working harder to achieve their subcontracting goals. Therefore, prime government contractors now need small businesses more than ever to help meet their small business subcontracting goals. The subcontracting goals are now being monitored by federal contracting officials, so the prime contractors are motivated to achieve the goals.

GSA SUBCONTRACTING

Even GSA encourages its Schedule contractors to subcontract some work to small business contractors. The GSA has a subcontracting directory available for federal contractors wanting to subcontract with GSA contractors. The GSA Subcontracting Directory for Small Businesses is published for small business concerns seeking subcontracting opportunities with GSA prime contractors. The directory lists large business prime contractors who are required to establish small business subcontracting plans and goals. The directory includes GSA large business prime contractors who have received federal contracts, other than construction, valued at over $650,000 and large business prime contractors who have received federal contracts for construction valued at over $1.5 million. The Subcontracting Directory includes the following information: Company's name and address, place of performance, product/service code, NAICS code, date signed, action obligation, vendor phone number, contract number, product/supply description, NAICS description, effective date, and the estimated completion date. The GSA also has eleven regional GSA Small Business Centers that help develop subcontracting opportunities.

ADDITIONAL SUBCONTRACTING RISKS

There are a lot of opportunities in federal subcontracting. However, there are also risks associated with federal subcontracting. If you are a small contractor performing the work for a large contractor, the large contractor may try to hire your valuable employees during or at the end of the subcontract. If your employees think that the prime contractor pays more, or if the prime contractor has a history of stealing small business employees, you need to beware of the risks. If you have a unique skill set that the prime contractor does not have, it may also present some risks. If the prime contractor learns of this skill set as a result of your subcontract, they may begin to view you as competition and refuse to subcontract with you in the future. You have then lost your competitive advantage in the marketplace.

Numerous small business contractors told me that subcontracting to a large prime contractor for very small companies is a risky business. However, if you are going to be a subcontractor, it should be a short-term solution in federal contracting. I have seen small business contractors and set-aside contractors receive multi-million-dollar contracts as subcontractors. Positioning yourself as a subcontractor increases your company's risks. If you can establish and build strong relationships with prime contractors and other subcontractors, your overall risks will be reduced and the rewards can lead to big payoffs in the long term.

SUBCONTRACTING PROCEDURES

Government contractors should follow acquisition processes and procedures, similar to those found in the FAR, when subcontracting work on existing government contracts. They must receive competitive proposals to the maximum extent practical for subcontracts. If awards are

187

going to be made without competition, there must be documented rationale to support an award to one contractor. If you are a prime contractor, certain FAR clauses must be included in the subcontracts. In addition, if the subcontracts exceed the subcontract consent thresholds in the FAR Part 44, subcontracts must receive the federal contracting official's approval before a subcontract can be awarded. Overall, the processes and procedures required to award your subcontracts must follow federal contracting guidelines.

PARTNERING THROUGH THE SBA MENTOR PROTÉGÉ PROGRAM

Another way to partner with other contractors is through the SBA's Mentor Protégé Program. If you have been a successful small or large business in federal contracting, you need to have as many contracting tools as possible. Regardless of the size of your business, you should understand the benefits of the SBA's Mentor Protégé Program. The Mentor Protégé Program teams 8(a) businesses with other successful federal contractors to give the mentor and the protégé an opportunity to receive government contract awards.

The SBA's Mentor Protégé Program helps 8(a) contractors to more effectively compete for federal contracts. The program encourages relationships among the mentor and the protégé contractors to help identify and respond to the developmental needs of 8(a) contractors. The mentoring program is designed to help small disadvantaged businesses. Small business owners can join the Mentor Protégé Program as either the mentor or the protégé. Large business can also be mentors.

The SBA will determine the eligibility of participants in the program, for both large and small businesses as a mentor or protégé. The SBA must also approve the Mentor

Protégé agreement annually. 8(a) contractors can only have one mentor at a time. The SBA will also serve as mediator of disputes between the mentor and protégé. The mentors provide the 8(a) contractors technical and management assistance. They can also form various teaming arrangements and joint ventures when competing on government contracts. Mentors can also provide equity and loans to the 8(a) contractors including owning up to a 40% interest in the 8(a) protégé company.

To be included in the Mentor Protégé Program, the 8(a) contractor must be in the developmental stage of the 8(a) Business Development Program and have never received an 8(a) contract. The 8(a) contractor must also be in good standing in the 8(a) Business Development Program and be current with all reporting requirements. The mentor can be a small or large business. However, the mentor must have the capability to assist the 8(a) company when necessary. The mentor must commit to the program for at least a year. The mentor must be financially stable, in good standing as a federal contractor, and able to provide support based on its experience. A mentor cannot have more than one protégé at a time without the SBA's authorization.

The Mentor Protégé Program can assist your company in gaining a foothold in government contracting if you are having trouble finding success. If you receive a five-year contract award with an agency through this program, the work can be phased so that the mentor is performing most of the work in the first year of the contract. As each year goes by, the 8(a) company performs more of the work. The SBA programs require that the SBA prime contractor must perform more than 50% of the work under a contract, but that 50% threshold is over the period of the contract, including options. Therefore, the experienced contractor can do 90% of the work in the first year to help you structure your business. This is a significant advantage for small businesses that need help starting. The phased-in approach gives a small company additional time to put all of the processes in place to learn how to run and manage their federal contracting business.

If you are a large or small business with no competitive Set-Aside Program advantages, the Mentor Protégé Program is also a benefit to you. It provides a company federal business opportunities that were not previously available. If you team with the right contractor, you can engage agencies that your company had not previously been able to access. A Mentor Protégé contract with a new agency can help your company gather information and build relationships at that agency. Go to the SBA website to find additional details regarding the Mentor Protégé Program. Entering this program provides your company another advantage in the federal marketplace, regardless whether you are a large or small business.

PARTNERING BY HELPING OTHER COMPANIES

I have seen one marketing technique applied in which a business development expert brought two or more contractors together to form a team on an effort that did not involve his company. Based on his knowledge of an agency's acquisition plans and contractor skill sets, he would recommend that one contractor work with another contractor, thus teaming them together to propose on an acquisition. As a result of his ability to do this, contractors trusted him and were often eager to contact and/or team with him. He had a great reputation because he helped others when it did not directly benefit his company. However, it did directly benefit him by building relationships with a lot of companies. This should be a strategy you should consider to help you build relationships.

Subcontracting opportunities must always be considered for all new federal contractors. Today, it is the best way to start your company in the business of government contracting. Without this experience, it will be difficult to break into federal contracting. However, you have to gather information and build relationships before you can even start subcontracting. Building relationships and gathering information are always the keys to success.

It is now a good time to be a subcontractor because large federal contractors have a more urgent need to subcontract a portion of their contracts due to the eSRS. However the risks in federal contracting remain. Pick the contractors you subcontract with very carefully, otherwise, you may regret it. If you choose carefully and correctly, it can lead to big dividends for your company.

An expert program manager with a targeted agency located in Baltimore recently told me that his capture consultants must be physically located in Baltimore. This particular program manager is an expert in business development and capture activities. He understands the value of developing relationships with both government and contractor personnel. It is very difficult to develop relationships if you are not physically located close to your targeted agency. If you are not physically located close to your targeted agency, you will not even have the opportunity to obtain regular access to the federal buildings. Also, in a smaller city, everyone knows the key players and if they are considered locals or outsiders. A local will have a personal track record among colleagues, while an outsider will not be well known. Being physically located close to the targeted agency will help you to effectively build relationships with other contractors.

The SBA has a website that assists small businesses in locating large businesses that currently have contracts. The SBA obtains the names and addresses on this listing from subcontracting plans that are submitted to the government when a large business receives a federal contract over $650,000. The listing provides the companies' names, addresses, and contact names by state. The listing is called the Subcontracting Opportunities Directory. The SBA's Subcontracting Opportunities Directory website is:

https://www.sba.gov/subcontracting-directory. Search the website link and determine if these contractors are located in your geographic area.

In addition to the Subcontracting Opportunities Directory, the SBA also has a tool called SUB-Net to help you locate large businesses looking for subcontractors. The SUB-Net database provides a listing of subcontracting solicitations and opportunities posted by large prime contractors and other non-federal agencies. It is located on the SBA's Subcontracting Opportunities Directory website. It is another tool used to gather information and build relationships.

CHAPTER 21

IS A GSA SCHEDULE CONTRACT RIGHT FOR YOUR COMPANY?

Is a GSA Schedule contract right for your company? The GSA Schedule is operated by the GSA. The GSA Multiple Award Schedule (MAS) contracts, also referred to as the GSA Schedule and Federal Supply Schedule contracts, are IDIQ contracts that are available for use by all federal agencies. Under the MAS Program, the GSA enters into government-wide contracts with commercial firms to provide supplies and services. When a GSA contract is in place, agencies can place orders directly to the MAS contractors. Each category of commercial products and services is called a Schedule. The GSA Schedule Program is therefore intended to provide federal agencies with a pool of contractors whose contract terms and conditions have already been negotiated with the GSA. It enables agencies to buy products and services in an efficient and effective manner, as opposed to the onerous full and open competition acquisition process. The GSA Schedule process saves the government and federal contractors both time and money.

The GSA products can also be purchased online through GSA Advantage. This is a great Schedule contract if you produce or sell products or deliver services listed on this Schedule. Through GSA Advantage, purchases for products and services can be made very fast. Contracting officers browse the GSA Advantage website's products and services. Once the products and services are reviewed, the contracting officer must compare features, prices, and delivery options. Products can be configured and

193

accessories can be added. Once this is completed, the contracting officer can place the orders online.

I have talked to a lot of contractors about the GSA Schedule, which seems to be a rite of passage for federal contractors to have a GSA contract. Most contractors think that when they receive a contract on the GSA Schedule, it means that they have succeeded. They think that it means they are competent in their field. However, being awarded a GSA Schedule contract is just one piece of the puzzle. Obtaining the base contract is the easy part. Receiving task order awards once you are on the GSA Schedule is the hard part.

THE GSA SCHEDULE CONTRACT

A lot of federal contractors have been awarded a GSA Schedule contract. If you win a GSA Schedule award, you receive a five year unfunded contract that lists the prices the federal government has agreed to pay for your company's commercial products and services. The GSA Schedule contracts may be renewed for three five year periods, resulting in a twenty year contract if all renewals are executed. The GSA Schedule therefore helps federal officials establish long-term contracts with contractors, and makes those contractors available to all federal agencies. Federal agencies in turn have a lot of GSA Schedule contracts at their disposal to buy the products and services. Congress has also granted state and local agencies the authority to purchase directly from some GSA Schedules. The GSA Schedule establishes these contracts at discounted pricing as a result of volume pricing. Funded awards are made in the form of task orders. Normally, only Fixed Price and Time and Material task order awards can be made. Cost reimbursement task order awards generally cannot be made off of the GSA Schedules, but there are a few exceptions. There is GSA Schedule contracts now that

194

allow for the award of cost reimbursement task orders. The GSA One Acquisition Solution for Integrated Services (OASIS) allows agencies to award cost reimbursement task orders.

GSA Schedule supplies and services are categorized by a Schedule Number. A Special Item Number (SIN) is further broken down for each GSA Schedule. Some of the GSA Schedule numbers and contract areas noted on the GSA Schedule eLibrary website are as follows:

- 03FAC: Facilities Maintenance and Management
- 48: Transportation, Delivery and Relocation Solutions
- 51V: Hardware Superstore
- 520: Financial and Business Solutions (FABS)
- 541: Advertising and Integrated Marketing Solutions (AIMS)
- 56: Buildings and Building Materials/Industrial Services and Supplies
- 58I: Professional Audio/Video Telemetry/ Tracking, Recording/Reproducing and Signal Data Solutions
- 599: Travel Services Solutions
- 621I: Professional and Allied Healthcare Staffing Services
- 621 II Medical Laboratory Testing and Analysis Services
- 65IB: Pharmaceuticals and Drugs - Includes Antiseptic Liquid Skin Cleansing Detergents and Soaps, Dispensers and Accessories.
- 65IIA: Medical Equipment and Supplies
- 65IIC: Dental Equipment and Supplies
- 65IIF: Patient Mobility Devices - Includes Wheelchairs, scooters, walkers.

- 65VA: X-Ray Equipment and Supplies - Includes medical and dental x-ray film.
- 65VII: In-vitro Diagnostics, Reagents, Test Kits and Test Sets
- 66: Scientific Equipment and Services
- 66III: Clinical Analyzers, Laboratory, Cost-per-Test
- 67: Photographic Equipment
- 70: General-Purpose Commercial Information technology Equipment, Software, and Services
- 71: Furniture
- 71IIK: Comprehensive Furniture Management Services (CFMS)
- 72: Furnishings and Floor Coverings
- 73: Food Service, Hospitality, Cleaning Equipment and Supplies, Chemicals and Services
- 736: Temporary Administrative and Professional Staffing
- 738II: Language Services
- 738X: Human Resources and Equal Employment Opportunity Services
- 75: Office Products/Supplies and Services and New Products/Technology
- 751: Leasing of Automobiles and Light Trucks
- 76: Publication Media
- 78: Sports, Promotional, Outdoor, Recreation, Trophies and Signs (Sports)
- 81: Shipping, Packing and Packing Supplies
- 84: Total Solutions for Law Enforcement, Security, Facilities Management, Fire, Rescue, Clothing, Marine Craft and Emergency/Disaster
- 871: Professional Engineering Services

- 874: Mission-Oriented Business-Integrated Services (MOBIS)
- 874V: Logistics Worldwide (LOGWORLD)
- 899: Environmental Services

The GSA Schedule has been put in place to help agencies buy products and services in an efficient and effective manner. One of the most important aspects of the GSA Schedule is determining which GSA Schedule contract your company should be on and how to price it.

To determine which GSA Schedule is best for you, I recommend you review the GSA website and the products and services noted for each GSA Schedule contract. The website link is http://www.gsaelibrary.gsa.gov/. Review the products and services on each GSA Schedule and determine if they are similar to the products and services offered by your company. If your products and services are on the GSA Schedule, review the GSA solicitation for that Schedule. GSA eLibrary and FedBizOpps contain the GSA solicitations.

Once you have determined which GSA Schedule is best suited for you, you must complete the representation and certifications described in Chapter 4. However, you still have to determine which GSA Schedules your targeted agency uses before you commit to going through the effort to become a GSA Schedule holder. If your targeted agency does not use the GSA Schedule that is best suited for your company, you are wasting time and money preparing a proposal. Once you have completed the representations and certifications, you are ready to submit a proposal to the GSA. Since March of 2011, GSA Schedule proposals must be submitted electronically though the web based application called eOffer/eMod. Hard copies proposals are no longer allowed. The intent is to simplify the solicitation

197

process. Picking the right schedule can have big payoffs for your company.

If you want to find specific historical information about GSA Schedules, the GSA Schedule Sales Query (SSQ) website enables you to access the sales, business size, and NAICS information reported by the Federal Supply Schedule Contractors. The SSQ website also allows you to select a pre-formatted report with your requested information. The reports generated reflect quarterly information for the current year and the past five fiscal years. It will help you determine how similar-sized businesses have performed using the particular GSA Schedule that you are considering. The SSQ website is https://ssq.gsa.gov/.

THE BIGGEST GSA SCHEDULE CONTRACTS

A few of the GSA Schedule contracts are the largest dollar contracts in the federal government. The GSA website states that the biggest GSA Schedule Government-Wide Acquisition Contracts include:

- GSA Schedule 70 contract which includes general purpose commercial IT equipment, software, and services.
- GSA Alliant contract which provides customized IT solutions.
- GSA MOBIS contract which provides management and consulting services to help federal agencies to meet program goals.
- GSA Schedule 871 contract which includes professional engineering services.
- GSA Schedule 84 contract which includes total solutions for law enforcement, security, facilities management, fire, rescue, clothing, marine craft, and emergency and disaster response.

Each GSA Schedule covers a different facet of government contracting needs. If your company fits into any of these contracting requirements, you must strongly consider submitting a proposal to become a GSA Schedule contractor.

THE GSA SCHEDULE ORDERING PROCEDURES

Some of the GSA Schedule ordering procedures have changed in the past few years. The GSA Schedule buys must now be placed on the GSA electronic Request for Quote (RFQ)/Request for Proposal (RFP) system eBuy, unless it can be reasonably ensured that quotes will be received from at least three contractors that can fulfill the requirements. eBuy allows federal contracting officials to request information, find sources, and prepare RFQs/RFPs online for products and services offered through GSA's Multiple Award Schedule (MAS) and GSA Technology Contracts. The ordering procedures are found in the FAR 8.405-1 and 8.405-2. Most GSA Schedule and Technology buys are now being placed on eBuy.

One very important aspect about developing your GSA Schedule contract, which many sales staff and companies overlook, is that federal contracting officers have some discretion when picking contractors for a GSA Schedule buy. The GSA Schedule ordering procedures recently changed, but continue to allow contracting officer discretion. The FAR 8.405 states that contracting officers shall:

Provide the RFQ to as many schedule contractors as practicable, consistent with market research appropriate to the circumstances, to reasonably ensure that quotes will be received from at least three contractors that can fulfill the requirements. When fewer than three quotes are received from schedule contractors that can fulfill the requirement, the contracting officer shall prepare a written determination explaining that no additional

199

contractors capable of fulfilling the requirement could be identified despite reasonable efforts to do so.

Contracting officers at some agencies have discretion regarding which contractors receive a GSA Schedule solicitation for their particular purchase requirement. Other agencies require that every GSA Schedule solicitation must be posted on the GSA eBuy website. For the agencies that do not have to post the GSA Schedule buys on eBuy, contracting officers have discretion to send it to as many contractors as possible to ensure that they will receive three proposals. If they do not receive three proposals, the contract file must be documented accordingly.

It is your job to have federal officials provide your company solicitations for the GSA Schedule opportunities that are not posted on eBuy. This is a big area and opportunity that is often overlooked by a large segment of business development staff. If you can build relationships and continually request for your company to be included on GSA Schedule solicitations that are not posted on eBuy, you may get lucky and receive a solicitation and task order award. Your undertaking is to increase your opportunities for those solicitations that are not posted on eBuy. This is a big method for you to be a step ahead of your competition.

THE GSA SCHEDULE DRAWBACKS

There are a number of drawbacks to the GSA Schedule. Federal contracting officials may want to provide an opportunity to known contractors who are not on the GSA Schedule, and may therefore ignore the GSA Schedule. Contracting officials may also be unfamiliar with the contractors on the GSA Schedule and decide not to use it. If an agency has its own IDIQ contracts in place, it will prefer their own IDIQ contracts before using the GSA

Schedules because they have evaluated and made awards to their pool of known contractors. In addition, they will receive a limited volume of proposals from known contractors using their own IDIQ contracts. If they use the GSA Schedules and eBuy, the volume of proposals received by an agency for an acquisition is limitless. The agency is also often times unfamiliar with almost all of the contractors submitting proposals. The GSA Schedules may limit the potential acquisition strategies for a lot of agencies because contracting officials cannot generally award cost-reimbursement contracts using most GSA Schedules. Only fixed price and time and material awards can be awarded on most GSA Schedules. This limits the use of the GSA Schedules for contracting requirements at many federal agencies. Finally, a lot of contractors have been on the GSA Schedule for years and have never received an award.

MARKETING THE GSA SCHEDULES

Many contractors have thrived on the GSA Schedules and receive awards on a regular basis. One particular contractor I knew was a contractor that graduated from the 8(a) Small Business Set-Aside Program. The company was still a small business contractor, and was having a tough time competing against medium and large sized businesses when full and open competitions solicitations were issued. However, the company was very successful winning GSA Schedule awards. This work was keeping the business afloat and was giving the company the opportunity to expand their business. This contractor did a good job of gathering information and building relationships with a few federal agencies. As a result of the company's effort to build relationships, agencies not only knew his company, but they also sent him GSA Schedule solicitations that were not posted on eBuy. Therefore, the company had the opportunity to compete with a limited pool of contractors and was successful in the federal marketplace.

I had a meeting with a contractor who I had not previously known. The CEO was interested in an 8(a) acquisition that I would be placing in FedBizOpps in a few months, and the CEO and his business development employee wanted to meet and ask a couple of general questions. I asked a lot of questions regarding their business, and found that the business development employee was very familiar with federal contracting. The business development employee had worked for the company for ten years. I immediately asked if he was familiar with the FAR 15.201, "Discussions with Industry before Receipt of Proposals." He told me that he was not familiar with this clause, which told me that he was unfamiliar with fully marketing the company's GSA Schedule.

To fully market your GSA Schedule products and services, you need to be familiar with the FAR 15.201. You need to help the federal officials determine how to buy your GSA Schedule products and services in an efficient and effective manner. There are too many GSA Schedules for contracting officers to fully understand what is on each one and how they function. Some contracting officials rarely use the GSA Schedules. The contractor personnel left my office with a greater appreciation of how to sell their products and services using the GSA Schedule. If you do not have the basic level of understanding of how to market the GSA Schedule, you will not be successful using it.

AGENCY INDEFINITE DELIVERY INDEFINITE QUANTITY CONTRACTS

When you gather information at your targeted federal agency, you will learn what contracting vehicles your targeted agency has in place. If the targeted agency does not have IDIQ contracts or Blanket Purchase Agreements in place for products and services that you offer on your GSA Schedule, you have the opportunity to sell your products and services to this agency. It helps if you educate the federal officials how to effectively use the GSA Schedule. In addition, educate them about your products and services. Find a way for them to buy your products and services in an efficient and effective manner using the GSA Schedule. If you find an agency in this situation, you should target them. If you see this scenario, you will have a better chance and opportunity to be successful. If the targeted agency has IDIQ contracts or Blanket Purchase Agreements in place, they may never buy products or services on the GSA Schedule.

DOES YOUR TARGETED AGENCY USE YOUR GSA SCHEDULE?

Before you obtain a particular GSA Schedule, check to see if your targeted agency buys products and services using the GSA Schedule. FPDS is the best source to find this information. Do not waste your time and resources getting on a particular GSA Schedule when it may not provide any value to your company at your targeted agency. If your targeted agency does on the other hand buy a lot of products and services through a particular GSA Schedule, getting on that Schedule will bring value and opportunity to your company. I talk to a lot of business development staff and company CEOs that have GSA Schedules in areas that do not compliment their targeted agency. They often have a GSA Schedule their targeted agency does not use. That is pretty shocking. It appears that they have not fully accessed their targeted agency.

On September 29, 2011, the Administrator of the Office of Federal Procurement Policy issued a

Memorandum that may significantly reduce federal agencies ability to award IDIQ IT contracts, with the exception of GSA Schedule contracts. Agencies must now prepare business cases if they plan on awarding agency IDIQ contracts. The case must be posted on a GSA website for 15 days to permit stakeholder feedback. Once the feedback is received, the agency must make a decision to proceed or cancel a new IDIQ procurement. The decision must be reported back to the Office of Management and Budget. After December 31, 2011, acquisition strategies for all planned Government-Wide Acquisition Contracts must be posted on the website. After Fiscal Year 2014, all new agency IDIQ contracts must be posted on the website. The consequence of OFPP's Memorandum guidance may be fewer individual agency IDIQ contracts. This change may cause federal contracting officials to use the GSA Schedules more often for their on-going acquisition needs. This change may also provide federal contractors more opportunity to propose on agency solicitations through the GSA Schedules.

The GSA Schedule is an important contracting tool available to your corporation to facilitate receiving federal contract awards. You must get on the appropriate GSA Schedule to insure that your products and services can be procured effectively and efficiently at your targeted agency. Educating yourself and federal officials how to use the schedules is a good strategy for you to consider. The success on the GSA Schedule may also rely on your ability to gather information, build relationships, and convince the government officials to include your company on a GSA Schedule solicitation if they are not posting it on eBuy. It will pay huge dividends in the long run.

CHAPTER 22

BECOME OR USE A RESELLER

There are large corporations that do not directly sell their products and services to the federal government. However, millions of dollars of their products and services are sold to the federal government. Their products and services are sold using resellers who contract directly with the federal government. A federal government reseller is a company that buys goods from a manufacturer and resells them, unchanged, to the federal government. You should consider being a reseller or contracting with a reseller to market your products or services to the federal government.

A reseller is a company that sells products and services on behalf of another company including software or hardware vendors. These companies may be called resellers, managed service providers, systems integrators, original equipment manufacturers, or distributors. Resellers provide opportunities for both the manufacturer and reseller to market certain products or services to the government. This relationship also provides resellers with access to products, discounts, and technical support that may not have otherwise been available.

There are a lot of resellers in the federal marketplace. If you are an IT company looking to market your company's products and services to the federal government, search for reseller companies with existing federal contracts that act as integrators of IT in federal agencies. Meet with them about selling your products to the federal government or to help you determine which other vendors in the marketplace can help to sell your

205

products to the federal government. Look for other resellers in the marketplace, and find out if they are interested in selling your product. They may be interested if their agreements with other manufacturers do not limit their ability to represent your products to the government. If you decide to sign with a reseller, do your homework first and make sure that they are experienced, knowledgeable, and reliable. The structure of the reseller agreements will vary. In most cases, the agreement is based on a group of products or services that the reseller is selling. In other cases, it is based on the physical location of the territory. In any case, it is still important for you to gather information and build relationships so that your reseller agreements are established with the right company to market your products and/or services.

THE GSA SCHEDULE PROBLEMS

The GSA Schedule is not for every company. There are large IT companies with hundreds of millions of dollars in federal government sales who intentionally avoid the GSA Schedule. They avoid the GSA Schedule because they have determined that the GSA Schedule would present a large disadvantage to their company. Instead, they use resellers to sell their products and services to the federal government.

One of the best reasons for using a reseller is to avoid the GSA Schedule. Contractors do this because all GSA Schedule contract awards contain a Price Reduction Clause, which states that all negotiations aim for achieving the contractors' "most favored customer" pricing discounts. All GSA Schedule contractors are therefore required to have pricing or a ratio of pricing that is equal to or better than those provided to their best commercial contractors. Many contractors do not agree with this mandate of giving the government an equal to or better price or price reduction on a contract/task order award(s). Many companies have been sued by the federal government because they did not adhere to this clause, and were penalized tens of millions of dollars. As a result, many companies avoid the GSA Schedule altogether.

The price reduction clause requires that the GSA be notified if a contractor awards a commercial contract at a price below the GSA negotiated price or ratio of prices that were in place at the time of the award of the GSA contract. Once the GSA is notified of the lowered pricing, the notification triggers the GSA to reduce its price on the GSA Schedule for that item. If you intend to be on the GSA Schedule, you need to have the adequate personnel in place who know this clause. They must know how to monitor your compliance with the Price Reduction Clause to avoid potential conflicts between your GSA contract and your commercial pricing methodology. The GSA audits random contracts to ensure compliance with this clause. If the GSA discovers violations, it will require that you reimburse them on a dollar-for-dollar basis for all products and services, going back to the date of the price reductions. Therefore, understand this clause before you place your products and services on the GSA Schedule. A lack of understanding may severely impact your company's bottom line.

I am familiar with a few large companies that use resellers to sell their products and services to the federal government. In one instance, a company uses a reseller with a sales force that markets both their products and services. In another instance, a company sells its products and services through integrated service providers that have contracts with the federal government. In both of these cases, the vendors are very large federal contractors, but are not on the GSA Schedule. Instead of selling their products directly to the government, they use other contractors to sell their products and services to the federal government, including through the GSA Schedule. They have been very successful using these techniques.

MANUFACTURERS STILL NEED SALES STAFF

If you are a manufacturer and plan on using a reseller, you will still need to have sales staff. The sales staff will still go to the government offices to help the government staff resolve problems, learn about new technologies, and work to market the product's competitive advantages in the marketplace. Companies market this way either with or without the reseller to increase their chances of successful sales. They never involve themselves directly with the federal government contracts.

A few years ago, I met a high-ranking individual from an IT company, who told me that his company started in the Chief Technology Officer's basement ten years ago. At that time, the company was selling over $100 million per year in Network Security Technology and was publically traded. I asked the individual how their sales had grown to such a large extent, and he told me that the products and services were sold around the world through resellers. The company did not maintain a direct government sales force, and were not on a GSA Schedule because they did not want to be stuck with the price reduction clause in the ever changing world of IT. If you are a manufacturer and are unfamiliar with the federal marketplace, you to need to think about how to maximize your company's sales using a reseller.

FIND PRODUCTS TO SELL

If you are an experienced federal sales person, you may want to consider finding products or services in which you want to be the reseller. If your company is an IT integrator in the federal government or commercial world, find products or services that are proprietary or unique and become the company's reseller. I would recommend that you take this step if you know how to sell to the federal government, or have established relationships with federal or industry officials, as it will give you a product to sell to your targeted government agencies.

Manufacturers use resellers to sell billions of products and services to the federal government each year. Whether you are the manufacturer or reseller, there are a lot of opportunities available to you. It all still begins and ends with gaining knowledge, gathering information, and building relationships. If you do this, reseller relationships can be used to sell products and services to the federal government.

CHAPTER 23

YOUR PERFORMANCE HISTORY

Your performance history is like your credit history. It includes a record of your performance in regards to government contract(s), and is very important in terms of your ability to win additional federal contracts. Like your credit history, if your poor history is reviewed by others, your future success securing government contracts will be difficult. Federal contracting officials are now required to formally evaluate your performance on contracts that exceed the simplified acquisition threshold. The official record of federal contracts is placed in a federal repository called PPIRS (Past Performance Information Retrieval System), and is used by federal contracting officials when evaluating proposal submissions. They are commonly referred to as Past Performance Evaluations. Past Performance Evaluations can mean the difference between you receiving federal contract awards or not. Therefore, it is imperative that you understand how your past performance is evaluated by federal contracting officials, what your role is in the evaluation process, and what you can do to improve your Past Performance Evaluations once they are reviewed by federal contracting officials.

The 1994 Federal Acquisition Streamlining Act (FASA) requires the government to consider a contractor's past performance in evaluating whether that contractor should receive future work. Section 1091 of the FASA, which is available on the internet, states:

> Past contract performance of an offeror is one of the relevant factors that a contracting official of an

211

executive agency should consider in awarding a contract.

It is appropriate for a contracting official to consider past contract performance of an offeror as an indicator of the likelihood that the offeror will successfully perform a contract to be awarded by that official.

The FASA required the Administrator of the Office of Federal Procurement Policy (OFPP) to "establish policies and procedures that encourage the consideration of the offerors' past performance in the selection of contractors." Specifically, it requires that the OFPP Administrator establish:

Standards for evaluating past performance with respect to cost (when appropriate), schedule, compliance with technical or functional specifications, and other relevant performance factors that facilitate consistent and fair evaluation by all executive agencies.

Policies for the collection and maintenance of information on past contract performance that, to the maximum extent practicable, facilitate automated collection, maintenance, and dissemination of information and provide for ease of collection, maintenance, and dissemination of information by other methods, as necessary.

Policies for ensuring that offerors are afforded an opportunity to submit relevant information on past contract performance, including performance under contracts entered into by the executive agency concerned, by other agencies, State and local governments, and by commercial customers, and that such information is considered.

212

The FASA also states that if an offeror of a federal contract has no contract past performance history, or the information is not available, they will receive a neutral rating.

All federal agencies are required to record the Past Performance Information in the PPIRS. The PPIRS is populated with information that is generated in the software application system called the Contractor Performance Assessment Reporting System (CPARS). Federal officials and contractors use CPARS to generate the data that is stored in PPIRS. Contractor past performance evaluations are generated in CPARS. When federal officials produce past performance history reports on competitive contracts and task orders, the system used to generate the reports is PPIRS.

The FAR Subpart 42.15, Contractor Performance Information, contains the regulations regarding past performance. It describes the processes required to complete the past performance information. The FAR 42.1501 states:

> Past performance information is relevant information, for future source selection purposes, regarding a contractor's actions under previously awarded contracts. It includes, for example, the contractor's record of conforming to contract requirements and to standards of good workmanship; the contractor's record of forecasting and controlling costs; the contractor's adherence to contract schedules, including the administrative aspects of performance; the contractor's history of reasonable and cooperative behavior and commitment to customer satisfaction; the contractor's reporting into databases (see subparts 4.14 and 4.15); the contractor's record of integrity and business ethics, and generally, the

contractor's business-like concern for the interest of the customer.

There are steps that must be completed for your past performance history to be stored in the CPARS. The first step that a contractor must take is to register in the CPARS. Contractors register in the CPARS through the SAM.gov. On the SAM.gov website, http://www.sam.gov, a contractor registers and must update their information profile to indicate a past performance input point of contact. In the SAM system, contractors can assign themselves a Marketing Partner Identification Number (MPIN) to gain access to CPARS. If contractors are already registered in the SAM, they will be asked for their DUNS number and Transaction Partner Identification Number (TPIN) when updating their profile. When logging in, PPIRS will ask for the DUNS number and MPIN to access information.

The next step requires the federal contracting officials to enter the basic contract information into the CPARS. Once the information is entered into the system, an email is automatically sent to the contracting officer's representative (COR), who generally assesses the contractor's performance based on quality of product and/or performance, adherence to schedule/performance, cost control/performance, management, and other areas.

Once completed by the COR, the CPARS assessment record is ready for the contracting officer to review. The contracting officer reviews and may provide additional comments to the COR's review. The contracting officer responsible for the contract completes the action in CPARS. Once this action is finalized, the CPARS automatically sends an email to the contractor's representative noted in the SAM. The CPARS automatically emails the contractor the contracting officer's preliminary

214

evaluation. The contractor reviews the evaluation. The contractor can submit a response accepting or recommending changes to the evaluation or do nothing. If no response is received in thirty days, the evaluations will be accepted as initially submitted by the contracting officer. A contractor's response to the evaluation automatically creates another email, which is sent to the contracting officer for review. The contracting officer may either change the evaluation based on a contractor's rebuttal or process the evaluation as it was originally submitted. If the contractor submits a rebuttal, the final past performance evaluation is forwarded one level above the contracting officer for review and is then finalized in the CPARS.

KNOW HOW YOU WILL BE SCORED EARLY IN THE PERFORMANCE PERIOD

Ideally, you should discuss the expectations of the Past Performance Evaluations in the first month of your contract. You need to meet with the COR and understand what it will take to receive the highest rating as compared to a satisfactory rating. I rarely hear or see this done by very experienced contractors early in the contract, though it is a very important part of understanding and receiving a high rating. In this early stage of your contract's period of performance, the COR is the individual who has the most influence on your score. You want to understand their rating methodology so that you can satisfy them. If you do this up front, you will not be shocked when you receive your rating. You should also have a similar conversation with the contracting officer, though they will probably go along with the COR's score if it is well documented. Do not wait until the end of your contract to ask a contracting officer or COR how the past performance evaluation will be scored.

HOW WERE YOU SCORED

Contractors must review the preliminary past performance evaluations in thirty days and either accept it or provide a rebuttal to the contracting officer's preliminary evaluation. This thirty day window provides your company with additional time to influence the preliminary review if you are not happy with the evaluation. There is discretion on the part of many CORs when completing the evaluation. For example, if you completed and submitted all of your deliverables on time, but not early, were you rated satisfactory or exceptional in the system? If you invoiced for all of the funding obligated on a cost reimbursement contract and did not exceed it, are you rated as satisfactory or exceptional? Various CORs may have scored you differently in the CPARS for similar performance. Ideally, you want the highest rating. In addition, consistent ratings by all agencies would help the past performance evaluation process. However, there is still not enough training of the government officials to make the Past Performance evaluation process consistent.

The FAR Subpart 42.1503, Procedures, contains the Evaluation Rating Definitions contracting officers and CORs use to evaluate contractor's performance. If you have a government contract, you must be knowledgeable of the FAR Evaluation Rating Definitions to fully understand and know how to defend your past performance evaluations.

If you receive a Past Performance Evaluation from the CPARS and are not satisfied with it, you have two choices at this point in time. The easy choice is to input a rebuttal into the system. In this case, the government's evaluation stands unless the contracting official reads your rebuttal and gives you a higher score. Your other choice is to call the COR or contracting officer and discuss with them why you think the score should be higher. This is the better choice, as it gives you more control over the process. However, do not let the thirty day period lapse before you make an official rebuttal in the CPARS system. Have a conversation with the COR or contracting officer and make this discussion calm and positive because your goal is to have continued relationships with the particular agency.

SUBCONTRACTOR PAST PERFORMANCE INFORMATION

The lack of a performance history in the PPIRS makes it more difficult for you to win a government contract. However, there are some ways to mitigate this problem. If you are the prime contractor submitting a proposal, you may want to consider subcontracting a part of the effort to a contractor that has a performance history in the PPIRS. If you subcontract some of the effort to another contractor with a PPIRS performance history, the government will evaluate the subcontractor's information in the PPIRS when evaluating your proposal. The government will also use other sources of information obtained from your references when evaluating your proposal. However, if you have positive information in the PPIRS, it may give you a competitive advantage.

DO NOT PARTNER WITH POOR PERFORMERS

Your past performance history is important. If you are proposing on a solicitation as a prime contractor or subcontractor, past performance of either party can play a critical role in winning the contract. If you are going to subcontract some of the work or be a subcontractor for a government solicitation, you may want to gain an understanding of your teaming partner's past performance history. If their past performance history is average or poor, you may want to reconsider the relationship. You may want to stop working with them on the solicitation, as they may reduce your chance of winning a contract. I have

217

seen contractors team and submit proposals with contractors with average and poor past performance records.

If their performance history is poor, it will be a major discussion point during negotiations. However, you do not wait to find out that your partner had a poor past performance rating during negotiations with the government. I see this happen often. If you find out during a contract negotiation, there is a strong likelihood that you will not receive the award. Therefore, plan accordingly. Review a teaming partner's past performance rating before you team with them. If you team with the right partner, it will potentially save your company a lot of time and money and hopefully win your company a government contract.

IS YOUR CONTRACT PERFORMANCE INFORMATION IN PPIRS?

The Past Performance Evaluations are not currently being put into the CPARS on a consistent basis at all agencies. I anticipate that the government-wide contract Past Performance Evaluations will eventually be completed in the CPARS on a more consistent basis. However, until all agencies use the CPARS consistently, the contracting officers may not have access to your past performance information in the PPIRS. As a result, if you have not yet had a Past Performance Evaluation on contracts that you have completed, government officials can request the contracting officer on your contract complete a hard-copy of the Past Performance Evaluation for active solicitations. Therefore, if you have completed one year of performance on a government contract, the past performance information can be used on solicitations even if there is no information in the PPIRS.

Past Performance Evaluations do become distinct discriminators in best value solicitations. Therefore, your

Past Performance Evaluation is very important to your company's success. Be sure to understand how your contracting officials rate your organization prior to evaluation being completed in the CPARS. Once the evaluations are processed in the CPARS, the federal contracting officials responsible for assessing your performance will be reluctant to change the rating. Once the rating is finalized in the PPIRS, your company's future success or failure may depend in part on the Past Performance Evaluations.

CHAPTER 24

GIVE THE GOVERNMENT WHAT IT WANTS

This book was not intended to help put a technical or business proposal together. However, based on discussions with a lot of contractors and government personnel, I believe that it is critical to provide one of the most important, yet simple perspectives in government contracting.

Government solicitations are often very complex, and contractor personnel can make the solicitation proposal process even more complex. Contractors often establish proposal teams to put their proposals together, and may over think the government officials' intentions in a solicitation. A very successful Vice President of a major IT corporation once gave me a good piece of advice in regards to this problem. I asked him what made him successful in government contracting, and he gave a simple response, "Just give them what they want."

This is a clear and simple statement. Government contractors often over think what the government wants. When you are preparing your technical and business proposals for solicitations or modifications, look specifically at what the government is asking for. Do not try to guess what they want. It should already be described in the solicitation.

This Vice President also told me that once you receive a contract award, your first meeting with the government is very important. He told me that regardless of what the contract stated or was included in the technical and business proposal, at the first meeting, he would ask the

221

senior program official, "Now tell me what you really want."

I am not advocating you do this. However, it is an interesting point of view to consider in your future endeavors. If your newly awarded contract has some inherent flexibility, you may also want to be flexible and give the government what it wants. It may pay big dividends to know what the COR, project manager, or program manager really want while adhering to the terms and conditions of the contract.

The federal government has hired a lot of new contracting and program staff over the past few years. Many of the staff have little or no experience writing statements of work, developing evaluation criteria, and establishing government cost estimates. Depending on the complexity of the products or services the government wants to procure, the odds are that the procurement officials' budgets were not approved until January or February. This means that they have a short period of time to write numerous scopes of work and evaluation criteria, with little or no past experience in doing it. Therefore, it is in your best interests to give the government what it wants and make the process easier, rather than over thinking the solicitation or a contract modification request.

Another senior contractor official I know retired and now works as a government contracting consultant. He was doing some consulting work for a particular client, preparing technical and business proposals for a large procurement. The client was trying to determine what the government was thinking when they wrote the statement of work and the evaluation criteria. He told his client that they were over thinking what the government intended in the solicitation. He told his client that the government officials do not over think the statements of work and evaluation criteria, and in reality, they have a tough time putting together the information contained in a solicitation. He told them that in general, the federal officials try to make the process as simple as possible.

I agree with these conclusions. Statements of work are sometimes haphazardly put together and proposals are evaluated by inexperienced personnel. They are inexperienced and often rushed to complete their requirement packages as a result of tight program schedules. They were not over thinking the requirements and you should not assume that they were.

Regardless of whether you are a small or large business, the federal contracting officials are no different than you. They are often under pressure due to tight time frames, inadequate staffing levels, or untrained staff. Sometimes they must push the solicitations into the marketplace without adequate time to contemplate how best to write them. As a result, if you are smart, you will give the federal contracting officials what they are asking for in the solicitation. If you do, you have a good chance of being a successful federal contractor.

CHAPTER 25

VIEW THE WORK FOR THE LONG TERM

Take the many techniques outlined in this book and choose on the ones that work best for you. Decide which techniques are necessary to help you win a government contract. First try using one or two of the techniques described in this book, and build on those with one or two more. Develop your marketing and sales plan with the proven techniques outlined in this book. Before you know it, you will be a government contracting and business development expert.

As was stated in the first chapter, government contracting is not for sissies. It is a tough business. You cannot wake up on Monday and expect that your company is going to start engaging in the government contracting business and have a contract by Friday. Even if you have a successful commercial business, you cannot wake up on Monday and expect to have a government contract by Friday. You must view the government contracting business as a long term commitment if you are to achieve success.

We live in an instant gratification society. Everyone wants instant messages, instant information on the Internet, and instant credit. Do not think that this will happen in the federal contracting marketplace. You need to follow the steps outlined in this book and build momentum. This momentum can take a lot of forms. If you are a new business, the most successful form of momentum is becoming a subcontractor. If you have been in business a year or two, winning that first contract is a big sign of success. Receiving a steady payment from a

225

federal contract helps you to stabilize your company and provides you with the basic means to be successful.

This book was intended to provide you with some of the information that you need to stay ahead of the competition. You need to continually gain knowledge, gather information, and build relationships to be a successful contractor. Other government officials may not share the points of view noted in this book, but these are key techniques that I have learned from being a federal contracting official for almost thirty-two years. The techniques noted in this book will help you get started as a new contractor, and may also help you learn new techniques if you are an experienced business development executive.

I hope that you are successful in achieving your professional endeavors using some of the techniques described in this book, but understand that this book is not the final answer. You must remain organized and develop a strong plan for gaining knowledge, gathering information, and developing relationships to successfully reach your federal contracting goals. I wish you the best of luck and success in your federal contracting pursuits.

?

Works Cited

Armed Forces Communications and Electronics Association. Jan. 2015. Web. 20 May 2014.

Association of Procurement Technical Assistance Centers. 2015. Web. 31 Jan. 2015.

Bloomberg Government. Bloomberg Finance L.P., 2015. Web. 15 July 2014.

Dunn & Bradstreet, Inc. 2015. Web. 31 Jan. 2015.

Federal Business Council, Inc. 2015. Web. 21 June 2014.

Federal News Radio 1500 am. 2015. Web. 21 June 2014.

Field, Lesley. Office of Management and Budget. Office of Federal Procurement Policy. Acquisition Workforce Development Strategic Plan for Civilian Agencies – FY 2010-2014. 27 Oct. 2009. Web. 21 July 2014.

Gordon, Daniel. Office of Management and Budget. "Myth-Busting": Addressing Misconceptions to Improve Communication with Industry during the Acquisition Process. 2 Feb. 2011. Web. 20 Mar. 2014.

GovEvents, LLC. Gov Events: Where Government Gathers. 2015. Web. 21 June 2014.

GovWin by Deltek. Deltek, 2015. Web. 5 Oct. 2014.

Healthcare Information and Management Systems Society. 2014. Web. 21 June 2014.

Professional Capture Management Forum. 2014. Web. 29 Jan. 2015.

United States. Congress. Jumpstart Our Business Startups Act. 5 April 2012. Web. 15 July 2014.

United States. Congress. Office of Management and
Budget. Office of Federal Procurement Policy Federal
Streamlining Act of 1994. 25 Jan. 1994. Web. 4 July
2014.

United States. Department of Commerce, Census Bureau.
North American Industry Classification System. 5
Nov. 2015. Web. 31 Jan. 2015

United States. Department of Defense. Defense Federal
Acquisition Regulation Supplement. Feb. 2015.
Web. 31 Dec. 2014.

United States. Department of Health and Human Services
FISCAL YEAR 2015 National Institutes of Health,
Justification of Estimates for Appropriations
Committees. Web. 13 Jan. 2015.

United States. Department of Health and Human Services.
Grants.gov. Web. 30 Nov. 2014.

United States. Department of Health and Human Services.
Health and Human Services Acquisition Regulation.
9 June 2014. Web. 31 Dec. 2014.

United States. Department of Health and Human Services,
Search the HHS Employee Directory. Web. 31 Jan.
2015.

United States. Department of Justice. The United States
Department of Justice Guide to the Freedom of
Information Act. 23 July 2014. Web. 31 Jan. 2015.

United States. Federal Acquisition Regulation. 2 Mar.
2015. Web. 31 Jan. 2015.

United States. General Services Administration. *Acquisition
Central.* Web. 10 Dec. 2014.

United States. General Services Administration. *Electronic Subcontracting Reporting System.* Web. 21 June 2014.

United States. General Services Administration. Federal Acquisition Institute. 2015. Web. 21 July 2014.

United States. General Services Administration. Federal Business Opportunities. Web. 31 Jan. 2015.

United States. General Services Administration. Federal Procurement Data System. Web. 16 Feb. 2014.

United States. General Services Administration. *GSA eBuy.* Web. 21 June 2014.

United States. General Services Administration. *GSA eLibrary.* Web. 21 June 2014.

United States. General Services Administration. Interagency Contract Directory. Web. 21 Sept. 2014.

United States. General Services Administration. *List of GSA Schedules.* 28 Jan. 2015. Web. 20 June 2014.

United States. General Services Administration. *Schedule Sales Query.* 17 Nov. 2014. Web. 21 June 2014.

United States. General Services Administration. System for Awards Management. Web. 31 Jan. 2015.

United States. Internal Revenue Service. 12 Mar. 2015. Web. 31 Jan. 2015.

United States. Internal Revenue Service. Apply for an Employer Identification Number (EIN) Online. 5 Jan. 2015. Web. 15 Sept. 2014

United States. Office of Management and Budget. IT Dashboard FY2016 Edition. Web. 31 Jan. 2015.

United States. Office of Management and Budget. USASpending.gov. Web. 31 Jan. 2015.

United States. Small Business Administration. Web. 31 Jan. 2015.

United States. Small Business Administration. Code of Federal Regulations, Title 13, Business Credit and Assistance. 12 Mar. 2015. Web. 15 Sept. 2014.

United States. Small Business Administration. Dynamic Small Business Search Database. 13 July 2004. Web. 31 Jan. 2015.

United States. Small Business Administration. *Subcontracting Directory for Small Businesses.* Web. 21 June 2014.

WikiOrgCharts. 2014. Web. 31 Jan. 2015.

Index

Made in the USA
Monee, IL
26 January 2022

89997999R00136